Eat Smart IN GERMANY

**How to Decipher the Menu
Know the Market Foods
&
Embark on a Tasting Adventure**

Mary Bergin

GINKGO PRESS INC

Madison, Wisconsin

Eat Smart in Germany
Mary Bergin

Although the author and publisher have exhaustively researched all sources to ensure the accuracy and completeness of the information contained in this book, we assume no responsibility for errors, inaccuracies, omissions or any inconsistency herein. Any slights of people or organizations are unintentional.

Map lettering is by Gail L. Carlson; cover and insert photographs are by Mary Bergin; author photograph is by Bill Lubing.

The quote by James A. Michener from "This Great Big Wonderful World," from the March 1956 issue of Travel-Holiday Magazine, © 1956 by James A. Michener, is reprinted by permission of William Morris Endeavor Entertainment on behalf of the publisher.

Publisher's Cataloging-in-Publication
(*Provided by Quality Books Inc.*)
Bergin, Mary, 1955-
    Eat smart in Germany : how to decipher the menu, know
the market foods & embark on a tasting adventure / by
Mary Bergin.
    p. cm.
    Includes bibliographical references and index.
    LCCN: 2012949015
    ISBN-13: 978-0-9776801-4-6

    1. Cooking, German. 2. Diet--Germany. 3. Food
habits--Germany. 4. Cooking--Germany. 5. Germany--
Guidebooks. 6. Germany--Description and travel.
I. Title

TX721.B47 2012   641.5943
                    QBI12-600194

Printed in the United States of America

To all the good people, especially
Midwesterners, who take pride in their
German heritage and are not quick to discard
the traditions of their roots.

Contents

Preface   ix
Acknowledgments   xi

The Cuisine of Germany   1
An historical survey of the development of German cuisine.

Early Beginnings   2
Charlemagne, Christianity, and the Crusades   4
Renaissance, Reformation, Resistance   6
Fairy-tale, Cookbook Lessons   11
Diversity in Diet   12
The World Wars   13
From Reunification to the Present   15

Regional German Food   17
A quick tour of German foods and their regional variations.

German Food in a Nutshell   17
The Regions of Germany   22
Southeastern Germany (Bavaria)   23
Southwestern Germany (Black Forest)   27
Western Germany (North Rhine-Westphalia)   32
Eastern Germany (Brandenburg)   34
Northern Germany (Schleswig-Holstein)   37

Tastes of Germany   43
A selection of delicious, authentic recipes to try before leaving home. Many are easy to prepare.

Shopping in Germany's Food Markets   75
Tips to increase your savvy in both the exciting outdoor food markets and modern supermarkets.

Resources   79

A list of stores that sell hard-to-find German foods, and of groups that offer opportunities for person-to-person contact through home visits to gain a deeper understanding of the country, including its cuisine.

Suppliers of German Food Items   79
Tours and Travel Advice   80
Useful Organizations and Travel Offices   81

Helpful Phrases   83

Phrases in English translated to German, with additional phonetic interpretation, which will assist you in finding, ordering, and buying foods or ingredients.

In the Restaurant   83
In the Market   85
Other Useful Phrases   86

Menu Guide   87

An extensive listing of menu entries in German, with English translations, to make ordering food an easy and immediately rewarding experience.

Foods and Flavors Guide   113

A comprehensive glossary of ingredients, kitchen utensils, and cooking methods in German, with English translations.

Food Establishments   135

A quick reference guide to restaurants visited.

Bibliography   139
Index   141

Preface

> If you reject the food, ignore the customs, fear the
> religion and avoid the people, you might better
> stay home. You are like a pebble thrown into
> water; you become wet on the surface but you are
> never a part of the water.
> —James A. Michener

When traditions turn into habits, they sometimes seem less precious with the passage of time. As a child, my family would eat bread at every meal, albeit the then-trendy Wonder Bread. No meal was complete without a buttered slice, and I thought little of it until doing research for this book.

No country produces more types of bread than Germany. *Brötchen,* pretzels, pumpernickel, *Zwieback,* and more—the country produces 500 types of bread. But this is about more than quantity: We're talking about a sacred product. German bakers long ago would not stand with their backs to the oven, because to do so would be an act of disrespect for the bread baking in it. It wouldn't matter if the oven was full of loaves of rye or communion wafers.

Friends grimace when I describe how my father taught me to dip a slice of plain white bread into still-hot bacon drippings, puddled in a cast-iron frying pan. The grease would soak in, and that bacon flavor was as comforting as any jelly or marmalade during the breakfasts of my childhood.

Whatever bacon fat was still left over would be drained into a cleaned tin can, to be used later in cooking.

Such frugality seemed normal for the times, but I didn't truly realize how much it reflected my own ethnic heritage. I am a mix of German and Polish descent, but I can't tell you much beyond that. I've shied away from researching family trees because the work seems more about lists of names than enthralling accounts of personalities and life stories.

But that bread-and-bacon thing drove me onto cultural tangents. When did you last buy lard? The U.S. home cook, if baking from scratch at all, most often resorts to premade crusts or crust recipes that use butter. The best bakers—including those in Germany—know it is lard that best adds to the tenderness and flakiness of pastry.

I also began thinking about bygone traditions, like plates of raw, ground sirloin as New Year's Eve appetizers at rural Wisconsin taverns. Spread a little on a square of rye or pumpernickel, top with slivers of raw onion, and add quick shakes of salt and pepper. We never added a raw egg to the presentation, although that is a tradition in some circles. Scares from *E. coli* and mad cow disease have obliterated this tradition in the U.S., but beef steak tartare has a long and proud history. What is French or Mongolian in some books was a German tradition to me, in rural Wisconsin.

This *Eat Smart in Germany* guidebook, like those from the 11 other countries that preceded it in the EAT SMART culinary series, encourages you to seek authentic foods and meals during your travels to Germany—or while at home, as you prepare the recipes that I have gathered from respected German chefs.

Eat Smart in Germany also provides practical information for traveling, such as useful German phrases, a glossary of food terms, and extensive menu listings.

About 50 million people in the United States consider themselves to be of German descent, more than any other ancestral group. What you presume about German food will depend upon where your ancestors lived, what traditions and foods they chose to value and pursue upon immigration, and how these customs survived the handoff from one generation to the next.

Guten Appetit!

MARY BERGIN
Madison, Wisconsin

Acknowledgments

Eat Smart in Germany contains the expertise and assistance of many people, and I am deeply grateful for their willingness and patience to share, advise, explain, and enhance.

For technical expertise, thanks to Brook Soltvedt for smart, sharp, and good-humored editing; Rose Stephenson of University of Wisconsin–Madison Continuing Studies for translation services; Susan Chwae for cover design; Nicol Knappen (Ekeby) for book design; and Gail Carlson for her role in creating this book's handwritten maps.

I appreciate the recipe contributions (all of which, regretfully, could not be used because of space limitations), cooking demonstrations, interviews and/or other assistance of these chefs, cookbook authors, other food professionals, and publicists: Herbert Beltle (Aigner Gendarmenmarkt, Berlin); Stephan Bernard (Le Jardin de France, Baden-Baden); Marcel Biró (Helms College, Augusta, Georgia); Susanne and Heinrich Breuer (Breuer's Rüdesheimer Schloss, Rüdesheim); Clemens Buchauer and Claus-Peter Lumpp (Hotel Bareiss, Baiersbronn); Thomas Bühner (Restaurant La Vie, Osnabrück); Lisa Cherepon (Maritim Hotels); Michelle Clasen-Werry (Clasen's European Bakery, Middleton, Wisconsin); Roz Denny (London); Anne Förster (Auerbachs Keller, Leipzig); Philipp Fouillé (Weinstube im Baldreit, Baden-Baden); Andreas Fritsche (Radisson Blu Schwarzer Bock Hotel, Wiesbaden); Brigitte Goertz-Meissner, Anne-Greth Paulus, and Marie-Lena Kuttruff (Baden-Baden Kur und Tourismus); Klormann Heilze (Gundel Bäckerei, Heidelberg); Dieter Jindra (Restaurant Gugelhof, Berlin); Grit Jossunek (Zur Pfalz Hotel, Hockenheim); Martin Kirsch (Linslerhof, Überherrn); Sylvia Knösel (Chocolatier Knösel, Heidelberg); Benjamin Kunert and Harald Wohlfahrt (Hotel Traube Tonbach, Baiersbronn); Ralf Kutzner, Dirk Schröer, and Birgit van Stipriaan (Bülow Palais and Residenz, Dresden); Ralf Leidner (Hotel Burg

Wernberg, Wernberg); Eva Mura (Niederegger Lübeck); Mary Niland (Mader's Restaurant, Milwaukee); Christiane Reiter (Rezidor Hotel Group); Jörg Sackmann (Hotel Sackmann, Baiersbronn); Thomas Scheinert (Schaubäckerei Scheinert); Jürgen Schneider (Strahlenberger Hof, Schriesheim); Alfons Schuhbeck (Schuhbecks Kochschule, Munich); Philipp and Anne Spengel (Zum Roten Ochsen, Heidelberg); Ludger Szmania (Szmania's, Seattle); Klaus Trebs and Monika Winterstein-Trebes (Gargantua, Frankfurt); Manfred Unger (Hotel Zum Ritter, St. Georg); Henning Weinheimer (Deidesheimer Hof, Deidesheim); Juan-Enrique Weinhold (The Cooking Ape, Frankfurt); and Renate Winkel (Cafe Maldaner, Wiesbaden).

My research in Germany was assisted by Lufthansa; Deutsche Bahn AG; Rail Europe; Steigenberger Hotels; eat-the-world tours; Wibke Carter, Victoria Larson, Tim Rosenkranz, Moritz Rothacker, and Katja Schnee of the German National Tourist Office; the European Commission's Directorate General for Agriculture and Rural Development, Document Management Centre; Corinna Born (Munich Airport); and tour guides Valeria Casagrandi (Baden-Baden), Peter Ferber and Martin Spantig (Bavaria), Susanne Fiek (Heidelberg), Laura Hoinkis (Hamburg), Manuela Junghölter and Eva-Maria Zeiske (Kiel), Madlena Kowar and Wolfgang Mendow (Bautzen); Jakob Krüger (Berlin); Jan Kruijswijk (Lübeck); Helga Kupka (Passau); Sandra Munivrana (culinary specialist); Annelies Paige (Wiesbaden); Ursula Wurzinger (Freising); and Susann Wuschko (Dresden).

Other valuable assistance was offered by Janet Brown-Lowe and Kelly Lao (The German American Heritage Center, Davenport, Iowa); Gerhard Fischer (Wisconsin Department of Public Instruction); Hartmut Holzapfel of Hesse; Stacey McNutt (Schiffer Publishing Ltd.); author Jim Pool of New York; Ivonne Przemuß and Ina Voigt (Friedrich Schiller University, Jena); John Schaefer (German Fest, Milwaukee); Isabella Schopp (Munich Tourism); graduate student Alyson Sewell (University of Wisconsin–Madison, Department of German); librarian Susan Stravinski (University of Wisconsin–Madison, Memorial Library, Department of Special Collections); and Arnim von Friedeburg (German Foods North America, LLC).

Last: Special thanks to the exceedingly patient, inspiring, and supportive Joan Peterson, Ginkgo Press publisher; and my steady guy, Richard Franken, who accompanied me during much of my research in Germany and was impacted by both my missteps and triumphs in the recipe test kitchen.

The Cuisine of Germany

An Historical Survey

Europe's seventh largest country, almost the size of Montana, does not lack diversity in its neighborhood or geography. Bordering the Federal Republic of Germany are nine countries: Austria, Belgium, the Czech Republic, Denmark, France, Luxembourg, the Netherlands, Poland, and Switzerland. To the north are the North and Baltic seas. To the south are the Bavarian Alps, where the highest German peak, Zugspitze, looms 9,721 feet above sea level in the Wetterstein Mountains.

Germany extends 7 degrees in latitude (roughly 47 to 54 degrees north) and 8 degrees in longitude (about 6 to 14 degrees east). Its widest east–west point is almost 400 miles, and the longest north–south stretch exceeds 510 miles. About one-third of the country's 137,800 square miles is the former East Germany. Of the 16 German states, Bavaria is the largest in size and North Rhine-Westphalia contains the largest population. Berlin (the capital since 1993), Bremen, and Hamburg are city-states, which means each is self-governed.

Slightly more than one-half of the nation's acreage is suitable for growing crops. An additional 30 percent is forests and woodlands. Ice Age glaciers from the southern Alps and northern Scandinavia shaped the country's regions: North German Plain, Central Uplands, Rhine River Valley, and Alpine Foreland. Marshes and moors, hills and lakes dot the landscape.

The Atlantic Ocean affects temperatures in western Germany, warming the air in winter and cooling it in summer. The east experiences hotter summers, colder winters, and more dramatic temperature shifts. A maze of five major rivers—Elbe, Ems, Oder, Rhine, and Weser—enhances the fertility of crops, although the sandy gravel of heathlands in northern Germany is of more marginal value.

The northern Kiel Canal that links the Baltic and North seas provides a crucial transportation link for freighters and other watercraft. Germany's central acreage is a blend of flat to steep terrain where anything from root crops to vineyards thrives, particularly in the Rhine River Valley, but the upland's rocky terrain and poor soil sometimes challenge farmers. In southern Germany, Alps foothills have an abundance of lakes, mineral springs, woodlands, and rich soil.

Germany is a part of the European Union and its 81 million residents have lived as one country since 1990, after the fall of the 11-foot-tall and 96-mile-long Berlin Wall, the concrete and grilled barricade built in 1961 to separate East from West Germany.

Early Beginnings

Before the start of farming, people survived as hunter-gatherers and typically followed nomadic lifestyles. Historians offer several theories about the origin of agriculture—defined as the control of plants for human consumption—but the definitive answer remains elusive because farm work began thousands of years before the invention of writing.

Near the Alps, well-preserved remains of almost 1,000 prehistoric pile dwellings and moorland settlements are protected as a UNESCO World Heritage Site in Austria, France, Italy, Slovenia, Switzerland, and Germany. These sites are as old as 5000 BCE and include various lakes and wetlands in Germany's states of Baden-Württemberg and Bavaria.

German archaeologist Friedrich Klopfleisch in 1884 concluded that agriculture arrived in central Europe between 5500 and 4900 BCE. Among his key evidence were distinctively decorated artifacts from the Linear Pottery Culture (*Linearbandkeramik* in German, or *LBK*), which was Klopfleisch's term for these first farming communities. Still unknown is whether *LBK* farmers moved to Germany from the Balkan states (Hungary and Slovakia) or if these farmers simply influenced Germany's Mesolithic hunters and fishermen to adopt basic farming practices.

The *LBK* were at home in Germany's Rhine and Neckar valleys about 5500 BCE, then in Alsace and Rhineland within the next 200 years. Their small communities typically were situated near waterways and contained simple wooden shelters for the farmers, whose harvests included peas, lentils, barley, wheat, flax, linseed, poppies, and crab apples. Fragments of ceramic *LBK* sieves suggest evidence of dairy production, with the sieves used to remove curds from whey in order to make cheese.

In large longhouses were livestock such as cattle, sheep, goats, and an occasional pig. Pork, throughout time, has reigned as a coveted part of the

German diet. But not until about 1500 BCE were pigs domesticated in Europe in what is now Italy and Germany.

Thin, fermented ales were brewed here from at least 800 BCE, and a tablet found near the city of Trier verifies the trading of beer commercially by the 2nd century. Sour wines also were being produced by the 2nd century, at Germany's oldest vineyards along the Rhine, and Roman teacher Ausonius was the first to describe the grape growing, in his 4th-century poem *Mosella,* which is a reference to the Moselle valley.

Roman historian Cornelius Tacitus, who wrote *Germania* at the end of the 1st century, described the Germanic tribes he encountered as barbarians and primitive farmers whose diet was little more than wild boar and other fresh game (fowl, deer, rabbits), wild fruits, gruel, curdled milk, and breads made from oats, barley, and millet.

Germanic tribes satisfied their hunger without elaborate food preparation and without delicacies, Tacitus wrote, and these simple meals were in stark contrast to the Romans' culinary gluttony and gusto for a more gourmet approach to dining. Tacitus also believed the Germanic tribes' penchant for fermented barley made them vulnerable: Supply them with as much of the potations as they desire, he wrote, and they "will be overcome by their own vices as easily as the work of an enemy." These were harsh observations, to be sure, but the prediction of weakness among Germanic tribes was inaccurate, as the demise of the Roman Empire in the year 476 proves.

Much later, others would offer glowing commentary about German character and values. Consider these excerpts from a 1789 essay about

An example of *Linearbandkeramik* (*LBK*) pottery, associated with Europe's first farmers. From the "Prehistorical and Early" historical collection of the Friedrich Schiller University, Jena.

German farm immigrants, later known as the Pennsylvania Dutch (*Deutsches*). The author was Dr. Benjamin Rush, a United States academic, activist, and physician known as the father of American medicine.

In settling a tract of land they always provide large and suitable accommodations for their horses and cattle, before they lay out much money in building a house for themselves. The first house is small and built of logs. It generally lasts through the lifetime of the first settler and hence, they have a saying, that a son should always begin his improvements, where his father left off.

They always prefer good land, or that land on which there are great meadows. By giving attention to the cultivation of grass, they often in a few years double the value of an old farm, and grow rich on farms, on which their predecessors, of whom they purchased them, had nearly starved.

They feed their horses and cows well, thereby practicing economy, for such animals perform twice the labor or yield twice the amount of the less well fed. A German horse is known in every part of the state.

The Germans live frugally in regard to diet, furniture and dress. They eat sparingly of boiled meat, but use large quantities of all kinds of vegetables. They use few distilled spirits (whiskey and rum), preferring cider, beer, wine and simple water. In their homespun garments they are likewise economical. When they use European articles of dress, they prefer those of best quality and highest price. They are afraid to get into debt, and seldom purchase anything without paying cash for it.

Charlemagne, Christianity, and the Crusades

Charlemagne in 802 united most of Europe into a single Christian community, but also dictated how to plant everything from herbs to vineyards and issued directives on the amounts of food to be used at every meal.

That means the influence of Christianity didn't just affect the average person's religious customs. It noticeably shifted the rhythms of daily life. The kingdom's edict to make customs and religion uniform meant that the foods of Germany differed little from others in areas with comparable natural resources.

Charlemagne's executive orders protected his passion for wild game by regulating hunting for the first time. Royal hunting rights superseded those of the individual, and it didn't matter who legally owned the property. To add further insult, commoners were required to assist the king wherever he chose to hunt.

These rulings elevated the status of venison as a much-desired meat, especially since peasants were restricted from eating it. The higher a person's status, the more meat he or she could legally consume, but fasting also became a church-mandated part of life. Dairy products, eggs, and meat were not allowed during Lent and numerous other times of year.

The feudal system required farmers to relinquish much of their crops, vegetables as well as grains. Subsequent epidemics and starvation were dismissed as divine punishment for human sins. For the poorest, eating meant little more than gruel. While nobles feasted on open-spit roasts, the working class got their protein from salt pork, sausages, and black puddings—foods made with less-desired components of the animals, including their blood.

Monasteries provided, for some, a medieval welfare system, with care based on proper foods and herbs as medicine. History shows these efforts were not universally appreciated. As an example, *halber Hahn* literally means half a rooster, but in Cologne it is just a slice of Edam or Gouda cheese in a rye roll. The name of the simple sandwich goes back to the Middle Ages, when poor people taunted well-fed monks by declaring, "Can't you see how well off we are, this is a half chicken!" as they ate their meager meals.

Blutwurst (blood sausage) earned the nickname "Cologne caviar." Royalty ate lavishly and flaunted *Schauessen* (foods for show), which were more about attractiveness in appearance than excellent taste. Entire lambs or calves, covered with gold or silver, were delivered to banquet tables. Cooked swans and peacocks arrived with gilded beaks, plus full plumage. Meals lasted up to five hours, with musicians and mimes performing between courses, but the lack of refrigeration also meant spoiled foods sometimes were served inadvertently to the wealthy diners.

Charlemagne died in 814, and by 843 his kingdom was split into three parts by his warring heirs. The boundaries resembled modern France, the Alsace-Lorraine, and Germany. The lack of a fixed capital in Germany slowly eroded the Holy Roman Empire's power, in favor of regionalism. By the middle of the 17th century, about 350 smaller units—an unusual mix of bishoprics, cities, counties, duchies, petty kingdoms, and principalities—reshaped Germany, politically, socially, and practically. Each unit had its own ruler and churches; some had their own language and currency. Differences in architecture, culture, and food were evident.

Regional cuisines, influenced by neighboring countries as well as communities, mushroomed. Consider the Polish influence in *Piroggen,* a ravioli with sweet or savory filling popular in Frankfurt. At Erzgebirge, near the Czech border, the no-yeast and poached *Knödel* dumplings have Bohemian roots.

More diversity in diet became possible after eastward travel during the religious Crusades in the 11th to 13th centuries exposed Germany to a wide range of spices that were brought back and woven into the diet. Sugar was introduced to German culture as a medicine and considered rare until commercial contact with the Mediterranean increased in the 11th century. When sugarcane crops and sugar production moved even closer to Germany, supplies increased, prices dropped, and the ingredient gained attention as a luxury food with aphrodisiac qualities.

As commercial trading gained momentum, the influence of Near East merchandise and dishes from other cultures—including French—became evident in German cooking. Examples include *Viande de Cipre,* sugared chicken with rice flour and almond milk, and *Saracen Brouet,* a spicy eel-cheese stew, both of which appeared in an early German cookbook.

Germans can thank the Chinese for indirectly introducing them to sauerkraut, a dish served by the barrel during the building of the Great Wall. The cabbage was soaked in sour rice wine at that time, and Mongols who invaded China brought the food with them to Hungary in the 13th century. Word of the fermented vegetable dish soon got to Germany, where it was elevated in popularity and remains a favorite dish nationwide.

Renaissance, Reformation, Resistance

The 13th-century establishment of the Hanseatic League, a confederation for trading and other mercantile activities, spurred commercial growth and worked to assure the safe passage of products in transit along the Baltic Sea, as far as Russia. The confederation was set up by northern German coastal cities and in the 14th century grew to 100 members, most in German towns.

Some imports—figs, cinnamon, nutmeg, ginger—enhanced the diet. Others, such as copper and iron from Sweden, improved the farmer's cadre of tools to plant and harvest crops. A new middle class, especially in urban areas, emerged with the prosperity of this increased trade.

Just as a guild developed for traders, so did fraternal organizations for nearly every trade and profession, to ensure the quality of work. These

Antique, wooden spice holder. From the collection at Spicy's Gewürzmuseum, Hamburg.

monopolistic guilds regulated many types of work activities, including the production and distribution of food. Berlin's guild for bakers, founded in 1272, required a baking test before membership was granted. Soon baked goods were being sold there for a fixed price. Rules often were strict. Bakers were not allowed to grind their own flour, for example, and kitchens were not do-all centers for activities from baking to boiling. A business kitchen likely would be set aside for roasting, frying, or baking—but not all three techniques. Cooks also could not slaughter animals.

For the working poor in crowded cities, who could not afford a home with cooking facilities, the *Garküchen*—commercial kitchen—was where to pick up and purchase a hot meal of boiled sausages or roasted meat. Some home cooks heated their prepared foods in a neighborhood oven, or avoided the need to bake by turning starches into porridge or pancakes.

German home cooking in the 14th century likely meant working around a fireplace with an adjustable pothook to hold a caldron of meats, vegetables, and maybe even fish. An alternative to these sometimes odd stews was to toast bread, fish, or meat on a grill at the fireplace hearth. Raw eggs were sometimes just placed on hot ashes, then removed when cooked.

Das Buch der guten Küche (The Book of Good Food) surfaced about 1350 and is the oldest known German cookbook. The contents verify an awareness of regional food differences and preferences. More than 100 years would pass before the publication of *Kuchen Maysterey,* the first printed German cookbook.

Much of what people in Germany and elsewhere ate during the Middle Ages depended upon their wealth and the compassion of their leaders.

A pothook holds a cauldron of meats and vegetables cooking over an open fire in this woodcut by David Kandel in *Kräuterbuch,* published in 1577. From the University of Wisconsin–Madison Memorial Library Department of Special Collections.

For example, after Maximilian I was crowned Holy Roman Emperor and King of Germany in 1486 in Aachen, the party was huge and generous. Oxen were roasted for all who gathered. Roasted lambs, fish, and rabbits were thrown from the windows of the palace where the new emperor dined.

The concept of salad was introduced in the 16th century, via Italy and the Alps, but only the wealthy could afford to dress it with olive or nut oil. Average people substituted vinegar or broth. Families ate at home, unless a village meal celebrated a special occasion. For weddings, an entire town might be treated to a series of free meals and tapped barrels of ale or wine.

The business of carving the main course at banquets turned into a test of skill and artistry. A good carver would use a fork to hold a roasted goose in place while slicing it with 20 strokes of his knife. Strasbourg woodcut artist David Kandel depicts some of these preparations for lavish late-night meals in the 1577 book *Kräuterbuch,* a study of botany, food, and foodways.

Although the Renaissance in the 15th and 16th centuries nurtured the blossoming of a new middle class in urban areas, the lack of an orderly system to ensure the succession of rulers brought Germany both regional freedom and turmoil. Voices of rebellion grew, and at the forefront was Wittenberg theologian Martin Luther, who pushed relentlessly for an alternative to Catholicism. The Catholic Church deferred to the Pope and his councils to decide what Christians believed, how they would worship, and the laws by which they would live. Luther argued for a separation of church and state. His 16th-century Reformation was a religious revolution that resulted in the founding of Protestantism, a move that roughly divided north from south within Europe, including Germany.

In response to the gluttony of the Middle Ages, more "sumptuary laws" (influenced by religious views) were enacted to discourage overindulgence in food (and a late 15th-century Nuremburg law even restricted fare at wedding meals). Protestant lawmakers frowned against eating in excess in public. Catholics were more concerned about what was eaten and by whom.

Since a ruler's religion dictated the path that citizens followed, migrations were allowed to ensure that a geographical area stayed peaceful and religiously homogeneous. German Protestants migrated south and food prices rose as the area's population increased. As meat became scarcer, the area's offerings of *Mehlspeisen* (flour dishes) increased. These dumplings, pancakes, and other starches are still served often in Germany, in both savory and sweet ways.

Meat was not scarce in northern Germany, but peasants rarely had access to tender slabs and instead were left with offal and the toughest cuts. Culinary ingenuity led to long periods of marination for these meats, the development of spice blends, and greater variety in sausage making with ground organ or other meats.

The Reformation's aftermath fueled the Thirty Years' War, from 1618 to 1648,

Preparations were lavish for late-night banquets, as seen in this woodcut by David Kandel in *Kräuterbuch* (1577). From the University of Wisconsin–Madison Memorial Library Department of Special Collections.

9

which advanced the separation of Austria from Germany, shattered the power of Germany's trade cities, and devastated its farmland. The country's population dropped from 21 million to 13.5 million, and one-third of the northern farmland remained dormant at least one generation later.

The conflict ended with the Peace of Westphalia, which established France as a power in internal German politics. Before this, the French influence on German cooking and baking was slight. Now French recipes began to be translated into German, and writers started slipping French cooking methods into German cookbooks. Even handwritten family cookbooks showed the influence of chef François Pierre de la Varenne, who was reforming French cookery. Among the innovations were refined desserts, including yeast pastries and *Torten*—delectable and light cakes that quickly gained popularity, replacing the long-predictable and heavily spiced honey cakes.

In 1685, about 50,000 Huguenot families left their homeland, in response to Louis XIV's growing intolerance with them in France. Some of these emigrants made the Protestant areas of Germany their new home and brought their French cooking techniques and recipe preferences with them. Frederick the Great of Prussia, whose rule over the German kingdom began after his father's death in 1740, was raised by Huguenot governesses. He preferred speaking French to German and took immense interest in what he ate, making notes about dishes served to him and then detailing to his chef exactly what he did and didn't enjoy. The king enjoyed simple foods but constantly demanded a creative use of spices.

But his meddling didn't stop there. The ruler tried to make his peasants grow potatoes, first by distributing free seed potatoes and instructions about how to plant them. The response was less than enthusiastic: the tuber was dismissed as tasteless, something not even a dog would eat. So then came Frederick the Great's threat to cut off the noses and ears of farmers who refused the decree to grow potatoes. Armed soldiers were stationed at farm fields, to ensure that the plantings proceeded. Also a motivator were grain famines in 1771 and 1772, which brought a rapid spread in potato cultivation, to feed animals as well as people.

Germany was late to take serious note of the potato. Frederick the Great's actions came almost two centuries after the tubers made their way from South America to Europe. Now Germans love their potatoes, and it is not unusual to see them strewn on the ruler's grave. The *Kartoffelmuseum* in Munich is devoted to potatoes in artwork; the *Deutsches Kartoffelmuseum* in Fußgönheim explains the potato's important history in Germany.

Fairy-tale, Cookbook Lessons

Brothers Jakob and Wilhelm Grimm, born in the 1780s in Hanau, were librarians with an intense interest in the origins of German culture and literature. They took seriously the job of documenting their homeland's folklore and legends, and in 1812 finished *Kinder- und Hausmärchen* (Tales of Children and the Home). The project took the oral tales of peasants and others and condensed them into a simple, short, and written form (although the original work also included almost academic footnotes about sources and story variations). Several of the brothers' fairy-tale subjects—Snow White, Little Red Riding Hood, Cinderella, Rapunzel, and more—became internationally known and still-popular bedtime stories for children. Most of their 200-plus stories do not ignore violence, hardship, or the wrath of God. Happy endings were the result of hard work, obedience, and making the absolute right choices in the face of adversity.

Food often wove its way into the plot of the Grimms' fairy tales, reflecting the values and lifestyles of average people. A simple apple, bread, or field of

Scene from the well-known Grimms' fairy tale, Hansel and Gretel. From the German American Heritage Center, Davenport, Iowa.

11

vegetables—not feasts or gluttony—would be mentioned as something to be earned and for which to be grateful. A lesser-known Grimms' tale speaks to the sacred nature of bread: A mother used her finest flour to bake a pair of shoes for her dead child to wear, since there was nothing more precious for her to give. But it is a sin to tread upon bread, so the dead child did not find peace in his grave until the shoes of bread were replaced with ordinary ones. The story accurately documents a 14th-century legend. It was even customary for German bakers of long ago to avoid standing with their backs to the oven, because to do so would be an act of disrespect for the bread baking in it.

Diversity in Diet

Peasants and workers also ate traditional dishes of kraut and bacon or lentils and peas as the 19th century progressed. German dishes became more as we know them today, and the French influence on upper-class meals remained strong. Emperor Wilhelm I even employed two French chefs, a move that was repeated in the kitchens of Germany's aristocratic houses.

A wave of 1.5 million German immigrants arrived in the United States in the 1830s to 1850s. They came for many reasons: to avoid German military service, to start farm life anew on cheaper land, to seek religious refuge. At least 50 German-language cookbooks were evident in the U.S. between this time and the start of World War I. One of the most significant was the 1840s *Praktisches Kochbuch* (Practical Cookbook) by Henriette Davidis, later described as the Julia Child of Germany. By 1904, 35 editions of her book had been printed.

What made *Praktisches Kochbuch* so popular, and why was it updated so frequently? Greater demands were being placed on home cooks and, according to the publisher's introduction, "Without any reference to luxury a greater variety of dishes is expected, owing to a general realization that this is conducive to a better nutrition of the body, and that such variety is often attainable with the simplest materials." One example is dumplings. The 35th edition of the cookbook included almost 50 dumpling recipes, for soups and fricassees, or to eat with a sauce or fruits. The same book also made room for "food preparations for invalids," an English–German vocabulary of culinary terms, and the conversion of metric weights and measures "to conform to those in vogue and best understood" in the United States, although the author's readership was spread globally, wherever German was read.

The author declared that "economy" was important to good cooking. "An extravagant use of sugar, butter and spices does not make your dishes any more palatable, but on the contrary, it detracts from what would otherwise be excellent food," she wrote. "Economy consists further in utilizing all odds and ends which can be used for our nutrition and finally in a practical disposal of remnants of dishes which have once appeared on the table and oftentimes make a pleasant addition to our bill of fare, when skillfully prepared in another form."

Davidis died five years after Germany's 1871 reunification under Prussian Chancellor Otto von Bismarck. During his reign, Bismarck set a tariff on imported grain and introduced the sugar beet as a primary agricultural crop. Farmers exchanged inefficient but traditional crop practices for more modern methods that involved fertilizers and inventions of the Industrial Revolution.

Regional styles of cooking and customs were afforded national recognition and acceptance. Industrialization improved the average lifestyle of the middle class, which meant more people could afford at least an occasional taste of aristocratic foods and foodways.

The World Wars

By the turn of the 20th century, the average German consumed 132 pounds of meat per year. To create meat dishes, Germans continued to stew, smoke, mince, and grind almost all of the animal: kidneys and lungs, heart and trotters. When food rationing began in 1916 because of World War I, the per-person cap started as 0.55 pounds of meat per week, about one-fifth of what was normal. A disastrous potato crop and brutal winter forced Germans for the first time to eat rutabagas, a food that previously was used only for cattle.

Alsace and Lorraine were returned to France with the Treaty of Versailles and Germany's defeat in 1919. Three years later the *Gummibär* (Gummi Bear) was born in Bonn, and the Haribo company that produced it had 400 workers by the time World War II began. It is but one example of survival in the face of grave conflict, challenge, and life-compromising situations. Candymaker Hans Riegel died in 1945, his two sons were captured as prisoners of war, and widow Gertrud valiantly kept the business alive until her sons returned in 1946. The company subsequently thrived, generating $500 million in annual sales at the start of the 21st century.

Inflation forced many in Germany's middle class to lose their savings and face poverty by 1924. The stock market crash of 1929 deepened unemployment rates, and the rising National Socialist Party used the vulnerable state of the nation to its advantage, under the leadership of Adolf Hitler. Hitler's prelude to World War II was heavy promotion of the fish industry and whole-grain bread production. Both were, in retrospect, seemingly innocuous steps in his aim to establish an expanded, homogeneous, and self-sufficient nation. The promotions provided new jobs that were desperately needed among the working class, and with gains in employment came a trust in leadership.

As Hitler's strategy turned more militaristic, Jews were at first ostracized, then declared the enemy. About 6 million were murdered or died in prison camps by the time the war ended in 1945. Their elimination also meant that Jewish foods vanished from Germany, and the nation still experiences a widespread absence of this type of cuisine.

After the war average food rations were at least one-third below the poverty limit. Many German cities had been reduced to rubble by Allied bombs. At least 9 million people in former German regions were refugees, and most resettled in rural areas of the battered nation. Because so many homes were destroyed, it was commonplace for families to move into methodically constructed apartments with modern appliances. That, for some, meant adapting old cooking habits and recipes to new technologies, but rations had them living on 900 calories per day, far less than minimal nutrition standards. Ration cards allowed for the purchase of basic necessities (bread, cheese, eggs, meat, sugar, and canned products) but product unavailability was another factor. To cope, many families who had the room raised rabbits as a protein source. The food supply remained unsteady until 1950, four years after American CARE packs of preserved meat, dried fruit, honey, chocolate, sugar, powdered eggs, milk, and coffee were transported to the fallen.

For almost one year Western Allies airlifted food and coal to West Berlin in response to Russia's blockade of the city until the Federal Republic of Germany was founded in 1949. Food rationing and price controls ceased one year later, but not the frustrations of average people.

In 1951, the average American worked 68 minutes to pay for 2.2 pounds of butter. The average West German worked almost four times as long for the same purchase. In East Germany, food rationing did not end until 1958, three years before construction of the Berlin Wall. While the wall stood, East German food supplies were uneven, unreliable, and often uninspired. The reigning Soviet goal of high production and self-sufficiency for the area seemed to ignore quality of life and access to basic consumer goods. It became customary for East Germans to buy whatever food was available, in hopes of later trading with neighbors for other provisions.

From Reunification to the Present

Germany's population was in a frustrating, tenuous, and somewhat futile holding pattern until the Berlin Wall fell in 1989 and federalism was restored. As a sharp contrast to East Germany, West German annual meat consumption had soared to 221.6 pounds per capita in 1989, compared to 143 pounds in 1960, and West Germans also set a record for alcohol consumption, about 27 pints per capita. As of 2004, a mere 5 percent of German men and 10 percent of the nation's women said they drink no alcohol. Daily doses of beer or wine have been a part of life since the Middle Ages, and today about 1,200 breweries produce about 5,000 brands of beer.

About one-half of Germany's land is used for farming, and the country is among the European Union's largest producers of agricultural products. The nation leads the European Union in pork production. Cereals, including grains and corn, are Germany's most common crops.

Similar to other parts of the world, fast-food restaurants and supermarket chains with their lower prices challenge the stability of family-owned grocery stores, bakeries, butcher shops, and specialty food stores. Seasonal, open-air markets for fresh produce retain their popularity, similar to the "buy local" movement in the U.S. The German government is aggressive in pursuing Protected Designation of Origin (PDO) and Protected Geographical Indication (PGI) labels for distinctive regional foods and food products, such as Westphalian ham, Lübeck marzipan, and Thuringian sausage. The designation ensures that similar products are not labeled this way in other parts of the world.

Ease of access to exotic ingredients means meals in Germany, especially in its most metropolitan areas, often have an international flair. Germany offers a melting pot of ethnic cuisines, like any other industrialized nation, and this sometimes makes it difficult to find traditional German food. Menus are more likely a fusion of cultures.

So a trip to Germany brings the potential for many pleasant culinary surprises and an unexpected depth of cuisine. Quality is not hard to find. There are about 250 Michelin-starred restaurants in Germany. That's at least 100 more than the United States contains. It also is a symbol of the great progress that Germany has made since Eckart Witzigmann of Aubergine Restaurant, Munich, in 1979 became the country's first chef to earn three Michelin stars.

15

Regions of Germany

 Northern Germany (Schleswig-Holstein)

 Eastern Germany (Brandenburg)

 Southeastern Germany (Bavaria)

 Southwestern Germany (Black Forest)

 Western Germany (North Rhine-Westphalia)

Regional German Food

A Quick Tour of German Foods and Their Regional Variations

German Food in a Nutshell

"The art of cooking, like music, is meant to give pleasure and to tide people over troublesome times." The quote belongs to Alfred Walterspiel, a highly respected German chef who died in 1960. The Baden-Baden native was best known for leaving a delicious mark on fine dining in Berlin and Munich. His sentiments reflect a universal truth, but it is one that is especially poignant in Germany because of the country's turbulent history.

This is a nation that understands independence, the lack of it, pressure to conform, rebellion, submission, pride, and survival. As the nation's boundaries shifted, split, and mended, Germans gained culinary influence from neighboring cultures, learned to become inventive with ordinary and limited ingredients, and stubbornly held fast to regional identities through their food and beverage creations.

The *gut Hausmannskost*—good home cooking—that defines Germany often involves butter, cream, egg yolks, and the rich sauces that begin with slow-roasted meats. It is similar with desserts: "A life without excellent pastry is possible but senseless," a tour guide in Wiesbaden declared, over a slice of delectable mocha-flavored cake with a vanilla mousse filling and coating of marzipan. We were at Café Maldaner, in business since 1859 and known for its longstanding ability to satisfy a sweet tooth.

Throughout the country, Germans tend to seek a sweet treat in the afternoon. The crumb cake *Streuselkuchen,* first made popular in central Germany, turned into a widespread national favorite. Desserts with poppyseeds are common in eastern Germany, and cake with pear confit filling is a favorite in parts of the Rhineland. Throughout Germany multilayered tortes of chocolate are separated by buttercreams, mousses, and fruit fillings. Most popular is the *Schwarzwälder Kirschtorte,* the Black Forest cherry torte with its fillings of cherries, kirsch-spiked biscuit layers, and whipped, gelatin-tinged creams. (See recipe, p. 65.)

Gastronomic indulgence with gusto seems to be a priority, no matter where you go, and food represents far more than sustenance. "Good food and drink are the sex of the elderly," the Wiesbaden guide explained, but "we are more active here. We walk, dig in our gardens, and ride bicycles" far longer in life than the average American.

So, hearty people and hearty fare. But how simple—and wrong—it would be to dismiss the German cuisine as a diet of sausage, kraut, bread, and beer or pork roast with potato salad and a glass of Riesling. In Germany are roughly 5,000 brands of draft beer, 1,500 kinds of sausage, 1,200 varieties of biscuits/cakes, 500 types of bread, and 13 wine-growing regions that produce 1.2 billion bottles per year.

It is true that a core of indigenous ingredients—including apples, asparagus, beets, cabbage, mushrooms, onions, potatoes, pork, and veal— define the typical German's diet, but within the country are regional variations and specialties that make menus much less predictable than the average traveler probably realizes.

Consider sauerkraut. It might arrive cooked with apples, citrus fruits, a broth, beer, or wine. The texture? Maybe crunchy and sour, maybe soft and sweet. The dish might be thickened with flour or grated potatoes. It becomes a condiment for sausages, a base for soup, a side dish to smoked pork ribs, and much more.

Variety in dumplings also stretches wide. They are made from potatoes, stale bread, or flour, plus eggs, cottage cheese, or milk. These doughy dollops arrive in soups, stews, and pies after being boiled, baked, or fried.

One version of *Labskaus*—pickled pork, anchovies, pickles, and beets—is nicknamed "sailor's hash." Another rendition of the rosy hash mixes mashed potatoes, onions, corned beef, cucumbers, beets, and herring salad. It is served with sunny-side-up eggs. In Lübeck, the mix is a beef, beets, and potato hash, with herring served on the side, and that distinguishes it from *Labskaus* in other northern Germany cities. In Hamburg, a related dish is *Lobscouse,* which is *Matjes* herring with a fried egg, gherkin, and beets.

So usually there is not just one official way to present a dish, and sometimes it is even hard to assign a particular recipe to a region because of the blending of generations and regions through the passage of time. This applies to many

A bread basket offers a medley of choices at Caroussel restaurant, Dresden. There are about 500 types of bread in Germany, made with a wide variety of grains.

popular German recipes, from stews to tortes. (And although the latter look luscious and sweet, they seem to have this in common: Few taste as overly sugared as they appear.)

German hams fit one of two categories—raw (cured and smoked or air-dried) and boiled (after curing)—but several subspecialties arise because of the cut of meat used, how it is flavored, whether it has a bone, and the materials used to smoke the pork.

Germany's vast range of sausages includes ground meats as well as organs: liver, lungs, and more. Consider *Sülze,* flecks of tender skull meat to which aspic is added. Although also known as head cheese, *Sülze* is a cold cut. Add blood to the mix, and the cold sausage is called *Zungenwurst.* Spice blends, type of meat, offal, other ingredients (such as blood), and texture, from coarse to fine, distinguish one sausage from another. So do appearance (small links of dried *Landjäger,* plump rings of *Lyoner*) and manner of production.

Brühwurst are sausages scalded in hot water or steam, and they require refrigeration after purchase. These fresh sausage links are among Germany's most common types, and a subset are the *Würstchen* that can be eaten hot or cold; think "frankfurter." *Kochwurst* are cooked sausages made from scalded or boiled meats or offal. They can be sliced or spread. The category includes *Blutwurst* (blood sausage) and *Leberwurst* (liver sausage), both of which were considered luxury foods long ago. *Rohwurst* are sausages made from raw

19

meat that is cured and hung in cool storage areas. These products, which are sliced or spreadable, include salamis and *Mettwurst* (a minced pork sausage).

Some circles place *Bratwurst* in its own category because of the meat (usually pork) sausage's popularity and range of regional specialties.

Sausage making, which began as a way to preserve meat that would otherwise spoil, today is a national point of identity because of Germany's longstanding high standards for quality and acknowledgement of regional variations. Contemporary chefs pride themselves worldwide in following a nose-to-tail philosophy that finds a way to use all of an animal when cooking. But such resourcefulness for centuries has been a part of the German mindset, especially during the leanest of economic times. If you were poor in medieval Germany, getting any cut of meat might have been considered a grand day; making do with the leftovers—carcass and beyond—was a part of daily living.

Sausages are meats for all seasons and meals. Germans bake their *Leberkäse,* fry their *Knackwurst,* add sliced *Fleischwurst* to pasta, dip into *Leberwurst* as a spread for bread, and snack on chilled links of *Landjäger.* They serve boiled *Weißwurst* with a fat pretzel for breakfast in Munich, grill finger-sized *Rostbratwurst* with kraut for lunch in Regensburg, and devour a mix of smoked *Pinkel* and kale for dinner in Oldenburg.

Most widely used condiment? Mustard. But it tends to be sweeter in Munich and carry more of a kick in Düsseldorf. Honey, vinegar, and horseradish are among the ingredients that add variety. The product comes packaged in jars or toothpaste-like tubes, and sometimes is a key ingredient in German sauces. A major German mustard producer is Bautzen, a Sorbian village near Germany's eastern border, but the industry employs only about 40 people because much of the manufacturing process is automated. Bautzen has a mustard museum, which has a collection of mustard pots and condiment sets dating to 1910. The Matthias Corvinus mustard, named after the Hungarian king who ruled this land in the late 1400s, is chile-hot, spicy, and the most expensive of the dozen-plus mustards sold at the Bautzner Senfladen Museum.

Butter is another popular sauce ingredient, but some German cooks prefer the flavor of bacon grease. Average families routinely add *Räucherspeck* (smoked bacon) to pots of dumplings and skillets of fried potatoes.

Germany's goose-eating season begins with Thanksgiving, and the use of goose fat peaks at Christmas time. The holiday bird traditionally is stuffed with apples, prunes, and herbs, but the mix usually is discarded after the goose is cooked. Goose fat, though, is saved; grated apples are added and then it is spread on bread or used to fry potatoes.

Germany's craving for *Hirschfleisch* (venison) is longstanding and widespread. It is popular on autumn menus and served as stew, roasts, or saddles of sauce-topped steak. Interest in this meat goes beyond hunting and domestically farmed deer. No country purchases more New Zealand farmed venison, for example, than Germany, which buys more than 40 percent of the Kiwi bounty. These imports are slightly more than the amount of venison processed from Germany's nearly 4,000 deer farms, most of which are in Bavaria, Westphalia, and the North Rhine.

More than one-half of the country's acreage is used for farming, and Germany is among the European Union's largest producers of agricultural products. Grains, vegetables, pork, beef, and veal are among the bounty.

Until the 1871 reunification under Otto von Bismarck, Germany was a mesh of many independent states, cities, counties, and kingdoms. Factor in climate and terrain differences, and it all spells differences in ingredient availability and food preferences. That means Bavarians and Berliners do not always understand each other in the kitchen. Baltic Sea communities eat more potatoes and fish. East Germans were raised on boiled sausages and kraut.

Cooks in northern Germany show a penchant for preparing fruits and vegetables together. Examples include apples with carrots or potatoes, green beans with pears and bacon or ham. Thick soups and those with fruit also are popular in northern Germany. Southern Germans opt for more broths to which some type of starch, noodles to semolina, is added.

Currywurst, street vendor fare that originated in Berlin, is a fast-food lunch consisting of sausage chunks covered with a spiced, tomato-based sauce. Like chili in the United States, there are many regional variations. East Germans use skinless sausage in *Currywurst.* It is a bratwurst in the Rhineland, covered with a thin and dark-red sauce. In Cologne and Düsseldorf, a comparable dish is the *Mantaplatte* ("white trash plate") of sausage pieces and french fries doused with a mix of ketchup and mayo.

And since it is not uncommon for some parts of Germany to have their own dialect and regional quirks, similar foods sometimes have different regional names. Hard rolls are *Brötchen* in northern Germany but *Semmeln* in Bavaria. A jelly doughnut is *Pfannkuchen* in Berlin, *Krapfen* in Bavaria. Dumplings are *Kloß* in the north, *Knödel* in the south, and also known as *Klopse* and *Dampfnudeln* (steamed noodles).

Boundary shifts from world wars added further regional nuances to German cuisine. Consider the influence of neighboring countries, especially Denmark to the north, France and Belgium to the west, Poland and Russia to the east, Austria and Switzerland to the south. *Piroggen,* a ravioli with sweet or savory filling, is similar to the Polish pierogi and found in Frankfurt. *Königsberger Klopse,* balls of minced meat in a white sauce, is named after Konigsberg, now a Russian city. The *Döner Kebab,* similar to a gyro sandwich and popular in Berlin, arrived with Turkish immigrants in the early 1970s.

Germany's traditional stews, soups, pot roasts, and goulashes are not hard to find, but neither do Germans limit themselves to the products and recipes that have long defined them. This nation is not an island, so expect restaurant choices—especially in urban areas—to be as international in scope as any other cosmopolitan part of the world.

Since the 1970s, new generations of German chefs have found ways to redefine their nation's cuisine in healthier ways. The world's "Capital of Cabbage" today includes novel and low-calorie presentations of the vegetable. The fermented version is matched with steamed fish, and it is simmered in a delicate soup that is garnished with slivers of ham. Or it may appear as a light side salad, combined with shredded beets.

Always significant are the distinct foods and beverages that are produced in Germany. The European Union protects the uniqueness of regionally distinct products by maintaining Protected Designation of Origin (PDO) and Protected Geographical Indication (PGI) registries. The PDO and PGI designations mean that *Stollen* baked in Austria, for example, cannot be marketed as *Dresdner Christstollen* (Dresden stollen), and ham smoked in the United States can't be labeled as *Schwarzwälder Schinken* (Black Forest ham).

As of 2012, more than 100 items from Germany were protected on PDI and PGI lists, which are maintained by the European Union's Directorate General for Agriculture and Rural Development. This total includes about two-dozen types of natural mineral or spring water, which are not included in the regional products described in this chapter. The first word in these product descriptions usually refers to the geographic area where the item is found. When more than one name is listed in a description, it means raw and/or processed products of a similar nature or name are grouped together under the same PDO or PGI. (Examples: mustard plants and mustard condiments, boneless ham and bone-in ham.)

The Regions of Germany

Germany has a temperate climate conducive to agriculture. The northern coastal plains have rich farmlands, and the south, traversed by the Alps, is heavily forested. Germany has sixteen states that have been arbitrarily divided into five regions for discussion of their characteristic foods.

Southeastern Germany (Bavaria)

When Americans stereotype Germany, the beer gardens and polka bands of Bavaria (and the adjacent state of Thuringia) are what comes to mind. But forget the dirndls and lederhosen. This traditional Alpine attire and jolly oompah music typically appear only at ethnic festivals and tourist attractions. The real Germany is multidimensional and sophisticated (but don't be surprised to see babies teething on soft pretzels).

Bavarian beer gardens and taverns are prime places for the locals to socialize, study, and talk business. Patrons are expected to buy beer or another beverage, but it is fine to bring your own food for an impromptu picnic. These popular gathering spots are sometimes at unlikely places, including a courtyard between terminals at Munich Airport. The area is one of the city's heavily frequented *Christkindlmarkts,* between Thanksgiving and Christmas, with an ice-skating rink and booths with seasonal crafts and treats for sale. Munich's airport is also home to Airbräu, a small brewery that also serves the area's breakfast specialty: *Weißwurst,* a white, bland veal sausage traditionally served with a sweet mustard, soft pretzel, and *Weissbier* (wheat beer).

Sometimes Bavarian cuisine draws on the riches of Austria. Prime examples are apple strudel, and the classic *Kaiserschmarrn*—pieces of pancakes with currants, served with warm and spiced plum slices. This treat has even been found at the sleek restaurants inside BMW Welt, the auto manufacturer's visitor center.

Regensburg, a UNESCO site 80 miles north of Munich, is home to the Salzstadel, a casual restaurant with the world's oldest sausage kitchen. The kitchen has been open in some form since the twelfth century, and the typical lunch is a half-dozen Nuremberg sausages, served informally with kraut and *Wurstkuchl süßer Senf,* a sweet mustard.

In rural areas, expect neighborhood taverns that serve food made with local ingredients. One example is Schlossparkhotel Mariakirchen, a 1515 castle with brewery in a town of 800 people. Meat comes from a butcher shop less than 3 miles away. Bread is made at a bakery less than 500 yards away. Cheeses are locally produced, too, and local farmers are among the clientele. The hearty fare includes sliced meats, potato salad, and Bavarian sausage salad—a mix of meat, pickles, onions, vinegar, oil, and chives.

Cold cuts, pretzels, gherkins in an afternoon spread at Schlossparkhotel Mariakirchen.

Gingerbread was invented in Nuremberg, and that means many gingerbread houses go up in storefront windows before Christmas. But the treat is not as straightforward as it seems. *Lebkuchen* are simply soft and sometimes decorated cutouts, spiced with cloves, nutmeg, and cinnamon. *Nürnberger Lebkuchen* has been baked since 1395.

Elisenlebkuch, also a specialty of Nuremberg, is much different because it contains no flour. These cinnamon-flavored macaroons are made of ground hazelnuts, confectioner's sugar, eggs, and finely chopped, candied orange peel. *Elisenlebkuch* is named after St. Elisabeth, Germany's patron saint of bakers and gingerbread makers. These crisp cookies are a challenge to remove from baking sheets, so cooks place the dough on *Oblaten*—crisp, edible baking chips that resemble communion wafers. *Zimtsterne,* almond-cinnamon stars, are another beloved holiday treat that got its start in Nuremburg. (See recipe, p. 67.)

The adjacent region of Thuringia is renowned for its low-fat sausages made with a spice blend that includes marjoram. Only finely chopped pork, beef, and sometimes veal are used; the majority of ingredients must come from Thuringia. In the village of Holzhausen is Germany's first museum devoted to sausages. *Thüringer Leberwurst* is a spicy pork-liver sausage that is sold fresh or preserved. The product is described as "probably as old as the Thuringian butcher's trade itself," "among the best-loved sausages in Thuringia," and almost every butcher sells it. *Thüringer Rostbratwurst* is a highly spiced pork sausage that is grilled. The oldest recipe, in the Weimar State Archives, is from 1613. Fans included religious crusader Martin Luther and writer Johann Wolfgang von Goethe, who mentioned it favorably in his work. *Thüringer Rotwurst* is a coarsely mixed pork-blood sausage that is sold fresh or in glass jars. The recipe has been handed down for many generations and is nicknamed the "Queen of Blood Sausages." *Greußener Salami* is sausage with a long shelf life that is a mix of beef and pork (including bacon), mildly spiced, and smoked with beechwood chips. It is a longtime Thuringian product. *Nürnberger Bratwürste,* also known as *Nürnberger Rostbratwürste,* are spiced pork sausages that are served hot and grilled. Production dates back to 1462. About 150 local butchers and six meat processors make the sausage—a testament to its widespread popularity.

Southeast Germany's other geographically distinct products include *Abensberger Spargel* and *Abensberger Qualitätsspargel,* white and violet asparagus that are grown in the "sand belt" of Germany, the rural Kelheim district, and chilled quickly after harvest. Stalks are cut and sorted before packaging. The Bavarian specialty crop is trademarked, a cookbook is devoted to it, and every year the region chooses an Asparagus Queen.

Schrobenhausen is home to an asparagus museum, and evidence of asparagus growing in this area goes back to 1851. The product was referred to as the "food of kings," and that helps explain the regional significance of *Schrobenhausener Spargel, Spargel aus dem Schrobenhausener Land* and *Spargel aus dem Anbaugebiet Schrobenhausener.* The stalks, slightly nutty in flavor, are sold peeled or unpeeled and harvested up to twice a day during the spring. *Spargel aus Franken, fränkischer Spargel,* and *Franken-Spargel* also earn PGI status in Bavaria's Franconia. The stalks are tender, low in acidity, and slightly aromatic in flavor. During harvest (which ends in late June), spears are cut with a long knife, with no severing of the plant below ground. This manner of growing asparagus dates back to the early 1700s, and of the area's many asparagus festivals, Nuremberg's is the best-known.

Aischgründer Karpfen is mirror carp, whose color ranges from dark green to grayish blue. The fish's firm, white meat is low in fat content, and the flavor is compared to fresh-boiled potatoes; it is not musty or otherwise unpleasant. The species has been significant in the Erlangen-Höchstadt area since pond farming began at monasteries there during the Middle Ages. In the Aischgründ is Germany's warmest aquaculture, which nurtures the fish, and in Höchstadt is the world's biggest carp statue. Festivities mark the beginning of the traditional carp season (in September), and some innkeepers keep a tank of carp to use in traditional meals for their guests. Candy makers sell carp-shaped chocolate and gum.

Altenburger Ziegenkäse is a soft, raw-milk cheese. At least 15 percent of the milk used is from goats raised in Saxony and Thuringia; the rest is cows' milk. Caraway may be added to this cheese.

Beer produced in Bavaria is *bayerisches Bier,* and Bavaria is home to the world's oldest brewery, Staatsbrauerei Weihenstephan, in operation since 1040. Bavaria has 700 breweries, and nearly one-half of all European Union breweries are headquartered there. Wheat beer was invented Bavaria.

Worthy of its PGI status is *Mainfranken Bier,* an assortment of beer produced in a specific manner in Lower Franconia. Beer producers united here in 1986, but this beer production method is centuries old. At least eight types, *Leichtbier* to *Schwarzbier,* are brewed and sold.

Münchener Bier gains PGI distinction, too, for beer produced with water from Munich wells. Cash payments for this beer date back to 1280, and the products continue to be "an economic and cultural mainstay" for the area. At least 17 types of beer, from *Pils* and *Dunkel* to *Doppelbock* and *Oktoberfestbier,* are brewed.

No other part of the world devotes a larger region to the production of hops, the key ingredient of beer. The raw product, *Hopfen aus der Hallertau,* bitter to aromatic, earns a PGI. The first written mention of this Bavarian crop was in the year 860. Annual hops festivals and fairs include the *Wolnzacher Volksfest* in August and *Mainburger Gallimarkt* in early October.

Bayerischer Meerrettich and *bayerischer Kren* are horseradish and grated horseradish to which vinegar, oil, and spices are added (the specific recipes are tight-lipped secrets). The farm product has grown in Bavaria since the mid 15th century, and much of the horseradish planting and harvesting is done by hand. Bavaria also is where the pungent *bayerischer Kren* horseradish mix is made.

Bavarian bovine breeding stock is exported globally and in demand because they demonstrate a high yield of both milk and meat. Some of these breeds are exclusive to Bavaria, and the most important breed is the *Fleckvieh,* whose origin is linked to stock from Switzerland that were imported in 1837. *Bayerisches Rindfleisch* and *Rindfleisch aus Bayern* refer to meat from cattle born and raised in Bavaria (typically in the Alps foothills). This Bavarian beef is used to produce *Münchner Weißwurst,* a veal sausage. Other favorite regional favorites made with *bayerisches Rindfleisch* include *Tellerfleisch* (a boiled beef), *Kronfleisch* (hanger steak), and *Bofflamot* (long-marinated beef that is seared, then simmered for hours).

Schwäbische Spätzle and *schwäbische Knöpfle* are names for an egg-based pasta that is firm to the bite, irregular in shape, and uneven in texture. Short and thick to long and thin pieces of dough (hand-cut, typically) are placed into boiling water. Fresh and dried versions of the product are sold, and it is a staple in Swabian cooking in Baden-Württemberg and Bavaria. The food began as an ordinary meal item eaten twice a day, but now it is a culinary specialty and symbol of regional identity. Cooks compete to set world records in dough cutting, and *Spätzle* is considered the Swabian national dish.

Spätzle is not to be confused with *schwäbische Suppenmaultaschen,* pasta pouches that are filled with vegetables or minced meat, resembling ravioli. Bavaria's Baden-Württemberg and Swabian specialty is sold fresh or packaged and may be boiled or fried before eating. Most butcher shops, meat manufacturers, and local restaurants sell versions of the product, which began as a Lenten dish but now is eaten all year. The *Guinness Book of Records* includes *Maultaschen* categories for product size and speed of production.

Southwestern Germany (Black Forest)

The states of Baden-Württemberg, Rhineland-Palatinate, Hesse, and Saarland dominate this section. The peaceful and picturesque Baiersbronn area is home to the highest density of Michelin stars in rural Germany. What inspires these and other Black Forest chefs to maintain such high standards? The terrain is a lovely and lush mix of woodlands, vineyards, and orchards. *Gelbe Bergplaume,* a plum schnapps, is a regional specialty. *Schwarzehüsse,* bourbon-tainted chestnuts, garnish both ice cream and saddles of venison. Many of the tender-meated hogs raised here turn into much-sought *Schwarzwälder Schinken,* Black Forest hams. Many of the sour cherries grown here turn into *Schwarzwälder Kirschtorte,* the beautiful Black Forest cherry torte that reigns as a nationally beloved dessert.

A classic recipe for Black Forest cherry torte is deconstructed during short cooking classes at Traube Tonbach, a luxury resort with a Michelin-rated restaurant that produces 50 at a time. The time-consuming recipe (see p. 65) goes home with students, who also sample the finished product. Torte instructions involve many little steps that are best followed in a precise order. The recipe includes a dense biscuit cake carefully cut into three thin layers. Then each layer is doused with *Kirschwasser,* cherry-flavored schnapps. Whipped cream is gingerly added to melted gelatin sheets, but not at too hot of a temperature, to enrich other torte layers. Traube Tonbach also serves a delicate and contemporary rendition of the torte, the Black Forest Sugar Ball, whose highlight is a pulled sugar orb that is filled with cream and topped with a spun sugar stem. It looks like a cherry and sits on a thin chocolate biscuit and a port-cherry reduction sauce, garnished with marzipan and pistachios.

Also in Baiersbronn is Hotel Bareiss, a property that includes a forest for hiking and a five-generation farm with two gardens. Chefs work with at least 100 local food vendors and incorporate meats such as venison and partridge into menus because of the area's fondness for hunting and wild game. On the sweeter side, the chocolate-cherry-marzipan Bareiss Cake is sold both at home and abroad; since 2011, fans have been able to purchase it online.

The excellence continues at Hotel Sackmann, a third-generation wellness retreat in Baiersbronn. Chef-owner Jörg Sackmann was asked to design a menu for Lufthansa's first-class passengers.

A dinner favorite among locals at nearby Baden-Baden, the internationally known spa and casino city, is *Saumagen,* which is a pork stomach casing stuffed with ground pork, potatoes, and carrots. After baking and before serving, the stomach lining is removed.

A little farther north, Haus des Weines in the small town of Neustadt primarily sells wines, but a line of locally made balsamic vinegars also is popular. A hit is *Engel kuessen die Nacht* (Angels Kiss the Night), which has a taste of wild cherries and is produced by the Doktorenhof estate, which can be toured. The business also produces balsamic vinegars that are infused with figs, ginger, and oranges. The region's other specialty products include fig mustard, white wine jelly, and wine jelly with hot peppers.

At Trier, which is Germany's oldest city, a filling, five-course meal at Danben Schnauss arrives on one plate: soup, fish, an entrée, salad, and dessert. In the Rhine River valley are the many grapes that turn into fine Rieslings, plus almond trees that blossom in late February or March.

And throughout the state of Hesse, *hessischer Apfelwein* is the drink of choice among apple lovers in the Rhine-Main region. This fermented and sour apple cider is bottled only in Hesse, and the primary ingredient comes from the area's many orchard meadows. It is poured from the

Classic and contemporary versions of *Schwarzwälder Kirschtorte* (Black Forest cherry torte) at Traube Tonbach, Baiersbronn.

28

Bembel, a stoneware jug or pitcher, to the *Gerippte,* a diamond-patterned cider glass. The drink's color is golden yellow, and its counterpart is the *Süsser,* a sweeter apple cider.

Apfelwein was a part of Charlemagne's era, but then consumption dwindled as wine making increased. Crop diseases compromised wine production in the 16th century, so *Apfelwein* resumed its popularity, first among home brewers, then cider-press houses. The oldest cider-press house that remains in Hesse is the 1779 Zur goldenen Krone, in Hochstadt.

Frankfurt am Main's Alt-Sachsenhausen district is home to dozens of *Apfelwein* taverns, where visitors either stand at the bar or sit on long benches behind wooden tables, sipping the beverage with or without a meal. *Abbelwoi-suppe* is an apple wine soup with cinnamon, served hot.

What do locals eat with *Apfelwein?* At the workingman's Apfelwein Dax in Frankfurt, the inexpensive menu includes 10 types of schnitzel—ranging from unbreaded versions to those filled with ham and cheese. For snacking: raw, ground steak with egg and capers (spread onto bread) and *Handkäse mit Musik* (see recipe, p. 46). This regional cheese specialty begins with *hessischer Handkäse* or *hessischer Handkäs,* palm-sized and hand-crafted sour-milk cheese made from cow's milk and produced on farms for centuries. The first sale of this type of cheese was recorded at a town market in 1813, and the Lahn-Dill district is the center of production. Tradition calls for the cheese to be marinated in onions, vinegar, and oil before being eaten on dark bread.

Also on Frankfurt menus: hearty *gegrillt Rippchen,* grilled pork loin ribs, served with fried potatoes and a salad; *Praunheimer Staudensellerie-Kuchen,* a celery pie served in autumn; liver dumpling soup and sauerkraut soup. Here and elsewhere, expect bakeries to showcase *Zwiebelkuchen*—an onion cake, like a quiche, but richer—as autumn arrives. The onions are strong in flavor, and adding cumin is an option to ease digestion. It is customary to eat *Zwiebelkuchen* with a new wine (which resembles a juice).

In every town, it is not difficult to find stories associated with food history or heritage. In Heidelberg, the Chocolatier Knösel is home to The Student Kiss, a chocolate candy with nougat crème filling and a dark chocolate coating. This is the food of courting. If a student accepts the treat as a gift, it's a subtle invitation to continue the pursuit of a deeper relationship. The sweet tradition goes back to the 1800s.

Less romantic, yet endearing, is Zum Roten Ochsen (Red Ox Inn), where beer-chugging college students also come to find German comfort foods, such as stuffed cabbage rolls with fried potatoes or *Sauerbraten* with red cabbage and dumplings. More refined but similar in menu is the Hotel Ritter, established in 1592, where some waiters have worked 30 years.

Maultaschen, similar to ravioli, traditionally contains minced meat and spinach. "In monasteries long ago, they'd hide meat in pasta so God wouldn't see it," a Heidelberg tour guide explains.

Heidelberg's twice-weekly farmers' market in Old Town is most popular for its strudels, made with a sweet dough and tart fruit (usually Boskoop apples). Follow the area's mountain trails to discover other charms and culinary curiosities of neighboring small towns and vineyards. Consider *saure Nierchen vom Schwein,* pig kidneys marinated in a Riesling vinegar, which is a specialty at Zur Pfalz Hotel. The simple Schriesheim inn is on a trading route that has existed at least since 1620, and the kidneys are served with *Spätzle* and a salad.

Lest you think that small town means ordinary fare, consider Schriesheim's celebrated Stahlenberger Hof, whose cellar holds about 500 international wines and is about as old as Heidelberg Castle. The first-course menu might offer terrine of duck and duck liver, served with a graceful carrot parfait.

Among the region's geographically distinct products are *Allgäuer Bergkäse,* a sheep's milk cheese that begins with animals raised in the Allgäu region, and *Allgäuer Emmentaler,* a raw-milk cheese that is similar to the acclaimed Swiss Emmental but produced with milk from cows raised in Allgäu. *Odenwälder Frühstückskäse* is a soft and spicy cheese made from cow's milk in Hesse since at least the 18th century.

Vegetables are celebrated, too. In spring, the *Salatkirmes* celebration in the Hessen town of Schwalmstadt commemorates the arrival of the potato. *Bamberger Hörnla, Bamberger Hömle,* and *Bamberger Hömchen* all refer to a small, finger-sized and crescent-shaped potato with a smooth, light-red sheen that disappears after long storage. The flavor of these firm boiling potatoes is nutty, and the flesh is yellow. The crop has grown in Franken since 1694. This type of potato is popular in potato salad because of its firmness. Cultivation is declining, compared to other potato varieties, because of the difficulty in harvesting the *Hörnla,* which is often done by hand because typical potato diggers would damage this curved tuber.

Filderkraut or *Filderspitzkraut* is a pointed white cabbage with fewer and finer leaf ribs than the typical round cabbage. The Baden-Württemberg crop, grown by monks more than 500 years ago, remains a specialty south of Stuttgart. The cabbage is mainly used to make sauerkraut, and Leinfelden-Echterdingen hosts the country's largest cabbage festival.

A treat for courting, since the 1800s, from Chocolatier Knösel, Heidelberg. The candy has a nougat crème filling and a dark chocolate coating.

From the island of Reichenau, a UNESCO World Heritage Site in Lake Constance, come three vegetables deemed regionally distinct. The first were the products of monks, around the year 840. The *Gurken von der Insel Reichenau* are snake-shaped cucumbers. *Salate von der Insel Reichenau* includes iceberg, Novita, Batavian, and cabbage lettuces. *Tomaten von der Insel Reichenau* are tomatoes grown on the island. Some of these vegetables grow in greenhouses, but more are harvested in fields.

Schwarzwälder Schinken is smoked, boneless, and dry-cured ham made from pigs raised in and near the Black Forest. The product also is known as Black Forest Ham, and the traditional recipe for it is centuries old. It is dark red, with an outer layer of fat. Production began generations ago. The curing, in climate-controlled quarters, lasts several weeks after the meat is smoked over pinewood.

Schwäbisch-hällisches Qualitässchweinefleisch is meat from a heritage-breed pig that has been raised and marketed in Baden-Württemberg since at least 1820. *Schwarzwaldforelle* is Black Forest trout, fleshy and white to pink in color. It is a stream trout or rainbow trout that is farmed in the clear waters of the Black Forest.

Fränkischer Karpfen (also called *Frankenkarpf,* and *Karpfen aus Franken*) is a type of mirror carp significant in Franconia, where monasteries have produced it in ponds for at least 900 years. Some innkeepers keep a tank of carp, to use in traditional meals for their guests. A regional specialty is fried carp halves.

The *Oberpfälzer Karpfen* is another mirror carp with PGI status; the species has been significant in the Upper Palatinate since pond farming began at a monastery there in 1132. Now the area has about 3,000 carp farms.

A quartet of beer products, *Reuther Bier*, is produced with artisanal mineral water in the northern part of the Upper Palatinate, where the brewing began around 1742. Two types of hops also are considered regionally significant: *Spalt Spalter* and *Tettnanger Hopfen*.

Spalt Spalter is a highly aromatic Bavarian product harvested in August and September. Some is grown in former vineyards, and although the growing area is among Germany's smallest for hops, it is among the finest and most traditional of the country's hops-growing areas. Geological conditions, and lots of sunshine but little rain, distinguish this type of hops from others.

Tettnanger Hopfen, hops known for their delicate aroma, have been grown since 1150 in the Lake Constance area. Tettnang hosts a hops festival, and every other year "hop highnesses" are selected to represent the product globally.

Western Germany (North Rhine-Westphalia)

The state of North Rhine-Westphalia dominates this region. "Home of Ham" is one nickname for the area, which produces the famed *westfälischer Schinken,* Westphalian ham, which is made from a hind leg of pigs raised to graze on the acorns of oak-heavy forests. The meat is lightly smoked with beechwood and juniper berries.

Pumpernickel also comes from Westphalia, and the word for this dark and slow-baked bread can be traced to a long-discarded local dialect. How long does the bread bake? About 24 hours, about the same amount of time that the dough sits to rise. These techniques are what cause the natural sugar in the bread's rye flour to darken and sweeten the dough evenly.

Other quirks of the area: Blood sausage topped with minced onions is informally called "caviar" in Cologne. *Gummibärchen* (gummy bears) were invented in Bonn in 1922. *Himmel und Erde* (heaven and earth) is blood sausage with sliced apples and potatoes.

Regional meat specialties include *Hämchen,* a cured and smoked shank of ham that is served with kraut and boiled potatoes in the Rhineland, and in Westphalia, *Pfefferpotthast* is diced beef that is braised with onions, seasonings, and broth before the gravy is thickened and flavored with lemon juice.

In the community of Burg is a monument to pretzel makers, who earned their highest level of fame in the early 19th century because of the high level of production. The few pretzel makers who remain sometimes let visitors watch the work. Another area specialty is *Zwieback,* twice-baked breads that have a sweet coating of chocolate or praline.

The region's other geographically distinct products include *Aachener Printen,* a type of gingerbread that might contain nuts (usually almonds) or be cloaked in chocolate, a glaze, or marzipan. The treat originally was sweetened with honey but now is sweetened with the syrup of sugar beets. The change occurred when honey became unavailable during a trade embargo forced by Napoleon. Even after French occupation ended, the tradition of sweetening foods with sugar beets remained. *Printen* gingerbread may have a soft or crunchy texture, and the other ingredients include cinnamon, anise, cloves, cardamom, coriander, allspice, and ginger. The precise mix is the local bakers' secret.

Düsseldorfer Mostert, Düsseldorfer Senf Mostert, Düsseldorfer Urtyp Mostert, and *Aechter düsseldorfer Mostert* are bright and creamy mustard spreads whose ingredients include triple-ground brown and yellow mustard seeds, a locally produced and unfiltered vinegar, mineral-rich water, and a specific blend of spices. There are no preservatives and the taste is hot, malty, and spicy. Germany's first mustard factory opened in Düsseldorf in 1726, and by 1884 Vincent van Gogh included the mustard in his *Still Life with Earthenware, Bottles and Box.* Before the century ended, the city had eight mustard factories, and by 1938 mustard products were being exported worldwide. Düsseldorf has a museum devoted to mustard, and many restaurants serve the condiment in special earthenware pots.

Mustard retains popularity in Germany, in part, because of the country's love of sausages. *Göttinger Feldkieker* is a firm, air-dried sausage made from raw pork that has been marketed under this name since the 1960s. The *Mettwurst*-type product is not of uniform width, which makes it different than the *Göttinger Stracke. Göttinger Stracke* is a firm, air-dried sausage made from raw pork that has been marketed under this name since 1980. The *Mettwurst*-type product is firm, straight and uniform in diameter. *Hofer Rindfleischwurst* is a finely minced, spreadable, uncooked sausage of lean beef and pork. It is cold-smoked on beechwood, lightly peppered, and not meant to be stored for a long time. Production began at one butcher shop in 1950 and eventually spread to involve other butchers in the area as demand exceeded supply.

The region's distinctive beer includes *Hofer Bier*, produced in a specific manner at Hof breweries since 1760, and the area's beer-brewing history began in the 14th century. At least 17 types of beer, *Schankbier* and *Eisbier* to *Kristallweizen* and *Weizenbock*, are produced. *Kölsch* is a pale, clear, and strongly hopped family of beer produced in a specific manner by breweries in and near the cities of Cologne and Bonn, where a brewers' guild was formed around 1250. Beer brewing began there in the 9th century.

Hop leaves sometimes cover *Nieheimer Käse:* a low-fat, high-protein, sour-milk cheese. The sharp and spicy product, made with dry *Quark*, sometimes contains caraway. It is a local specialty that has been produced for centuries, and it one of the country's few "original German" cheeses.

Rheinisches Apfelkraut is a thick syrup made from locally harvested and stewed apples and pears. The sweet, jelly-like Rhineland product is made from only the juice of the fruit, although sugar and pectin may be added. The product traditionally was used to sweeten food during harsh winters. Now it is a baking and cooking ingredient throughout the year. It accompanies *Rievkooche,* potato cakes that are a longtime regional specialty.

Rheinisches Rübenkraut, rheinisches Zuckerrübenkraut, and *rheinisches Zuckerrübensirup* refer to pure, concentrated, sugar-beet juice that is dark brown, sweet, and malty in taste. It is produced during the beet-harvesting season, late summer to spring, throughout the Rhineland. The process of transforming sweet, white beets into syrup is a centuries-old tradition still used today. Beets were one of the few items that farmers could use to pay landlords in the 15th century. By 1860, just the Grevenbroich area had 300-plus syrup producers. The Lower Rhine is the center of production today; beet syrup is a common ingredient in many Rhinish recipes, *rheinisher Sauerbraten* (marinated beef) to *Aachener Printen* (gingerbread).

Eastern Germany (Brandenburg)

The states of Brandenburg, Berlin, Mecklenburg-Vorpommem, Saxony, and Saxony-Anhalt dominate this section. Berlin is home to the *Grune Woche,* Germany's biggest agricultural fair, and that makes sense because of the Capitol City's proximity to fine vegetable growing. About 60 miles southeast of Berlin is the Spreewald region, known for its fertile farming. The *Spreewälder Gurken* are pickles made from gherkins grown in the Brandenberg area. The recipe includes onions, dill, other herbs or horseradish. The brine is sweetened with sugar. Another regional specialty is *Spreewälder Meerrettich,* horseradish grown organically in the Brandenburg area, then grated and bottled with vegetable oil and preservatives. During World War I, the Spreewald was the only source of onions for Germany. Onions used to be so important that legal contracts were drawn to make sure parents received their share after family farm ownership was transferred to the next generation. The three-day Onion Market held in Weimar in mid-October celebrates about 360 years of onion production. The event draws more than 500 vendors and about 350,000 visitors, making it the biggest festival in the Thuringia region.

In Berlin, a *Currywurst* museum opened in 2009 as a tribute to the city's favorite and inexpensive street-vendor food. The attraction is interactive and especially fun for children. It demonstrates the affection Berliners have for this fast food, which has been serenaded in music, movies, and prose. *Currywurst* is sold at almost any time of day, and customers often stand while eating it with a roll or french fries dipped in mayo. Herta Heuver was the first to sell the food, in 1949, as a simple meal that was a consequence of food rationing. Two years later she patented her sauce, *Chillup*—a mix of tomato paste and up to one dozen spices. Berlin's other popular street food is the *Döner Kebab,* a gyro-like sandwich that is garnished with assorted pickled vegetables. It has Turkish roots.

During the leanest of economic times, a Berlin tour guide says cow udder schnitzel was commonplace. For sit-down meals today, a favorite entree is *ofenfrische Schwein Shax* (pork knuckles, typically served with pickled cabbage and potato dumplings). Another comfort food is *Bäckeoffe,* marinated beef, pork, and lamb stewed in an earthenware pot. (See recipe, p. 54.)

Hirschgoulasch, venison goulash, recognizes the autumn hunting season and might be accompanied by *Spätzle* and cranberries. A popular spring dish is a mix of white asparagus and potatoes.

Good all year is a visit to Berlin's Fassbender and Rausch, a longtime chocolate maker with an upstairs cafe and chocolate menu of hot drinks.

The Elbe River separates old and new parts of Dresden, which is home to Radeberger, an 1872 brewery that was Germany's first to make beer in the traditional pilsner manner. Since 1992, a Saxon wine road has stretched 35 miles along the Elbe River, even though only 5 percent of the country's wine is made here. Ninety percent of Germany's dry white wines come from Saxony and much of it is grown in the Elbe Hills and riverbanks. There is too little sunshine to make much red wine, but about 7,000 bottles of white Merlot are produced annually. Merlot is the country's second most popular and harvested wine, after Riesling.

Also in Dresden is Caroussel, a Michelin-rated restaurant that has ranked among the top 50 in Germany. The menu emphasizes the use of local ingredients in unusual ways. So foie gras might arrive with a Coca-Cola glacè topping and lemon sorbet. Shrimp is paired with curry sauce and cauliflower. White bass gets a pumpkin sauce in autumn. This Relais & Chateaux hotel property also has a more casual bistro with a lighter or creative take on traditional fare. That sometimes means not using flour in sauces. For example, marinated beef might involve veal and caramelized sugar, with gingerbread and dark bread to thicken the gravy.

Southeast of Berlin, the Sorbian culture of Bautzen is endangered because only about one-half of the 60,000 Sorbs still speak the language and stay true to their culture. A pleasantly fierce core of residents fights to keep traditions alive. At the inn Wjelbik, female servers wear traditional garb that indicates their generation and whether they are married. A traditional meal begins with *Kwasna Poliwka,* a soup of meatballs, eggs, and slivered carrots. (See recipe, p. 51.) Then comes *Mjasom,* beef in horseradish sauce with a topping of grated horseradish. The entrée is accompanied by rye bread, boiled potatoes, and other vegetables. Dessert resembles a *panna cotta* with marshmallows, aswim in a watery berry sauce that has a slight mint taste.

The region's geographically distinct products include *Dresdner Christstollen, Dresdner Stollen,* and *Dresdner Weihnachtsstollen,* all references to a buttery yeast bread with a specific percentage of rum, almonds, raisins, and candied orange and/or lemon peel. It is dusted with powdered sugar. The tradition began in the 15th century, when the bread was baked for Dresden's Christmas market. The product remains popular during this holiday season; about two million loaves are sold and shipped globally each year. Baking begins in early autumn, and customers are advised to let fresh *Stollen* rest at least six weeks before being eaten. The stollen can last until Easter, if kept in a cool place. This is one of Saxony's biggest exports, and only 150 bakeries are allowed to market their product as Dresden stollen. All use flour, water, and yeast, but the spice mix is what adds variation and intrigue.

Other regionally distinctive products include *Eichsfelder Feldgieker* and *Eichsfelder Feldkieker,* which both refer to an uncooked sausage made from high-quality cuts of pork that are processed while still warm from slaughter. (Sausage typically is made with cold meats.) It is air-dried, firm, and pear-shaped. Production occurs in central Germany, in parts of Thuringia, Lower Saxony, and Hessen. These sausages have been produced since 1724 and have been favorably mentioned in numerous literary works.

Greußener Salami is a sausage with a long shelf life that is a mix of beef and pork (including bacon), mildly spiced and smoked with beechwood chips. The Thuringian product is made with an old recipe. *Halberstädter Würstchen* is a long, thin boiling sausage that is smoked in several phases. It represents a century-old tradition that began with butcher Friedrich Heine, who later opened a sausage factory and started preserving his product in tins in 1896. When his new sausage company opened in 1913, it was considered the biggest and most modern in Europe. Now several tons of this long-popular product are made daily.

Sweets by the box at Fassbender and Rausch, Berlin. Also available: chocolate drinks.

The area's specialty beverages include *Kulmbacher Bier,* an assortment of beer produced in a specific manner with natural spring water. At least 13 types of beer, low-alcohol to *Festbier,* are sold. Production began at a monastery in 1349. In addition, *Wernesgrüner Bier* is a pilsner beer made in the same village for at least 500 years. It has earned gold medals in beer competitions since 1896.

The eastern part of Germany also is known for *Lausitzer Leinöl,* a natural (no additives), nutty linseed oil, produced since the 18th century, and *Meißner Fummel,* a delicate, buttery, nonperishable pastry that is hollow and shaped like a little bread loaf. It has been baked in Saxony since about 1710.

Northern Germany (Schleswig-Holstein)

The states of Schleswig-Holstein, Hamburg, Bremen, and Lower Saxony are included in this region. Much about the northern diet makes it different from the rest of Germany. This area savors seafood, particularly herring and smoked eel, plus lobster from the rocky little island of Helgoland. This is thanks to northern Germany's proximity to the North and Baltic seas.

Matjes, a bun with marinated herring fillet inside, is very popular here. The cold, marinated fillets also might be served atop dark and nutty buttered bread with thick rings of raw onion and a garnish of cucumber and tomato. A Holstein-style version comes with a pickle, apples, onions, chives, potatoes, and salad.

The herring harvest is January to mid-May, with no limit on the number that can be caught. "It's as much as the fish want to come," a Kiel tour guide says. Salmon, plaice, flounder, cod, and rosefish also are caught.

Babies born in the port city of Kiel are automatically nicknamed *Sprat,* which is a type of herring harvested there. Each child is taught to swim and is exposed to sailing as early as 6 years of age. Pirate-themed birthday parties are not unusual. Sailing camps are well-attended in summer. "We have a lot of steady wind for sailing but calmness in our bay," the tour guide explains, and the annual Kiel Week in summer is the world's largest sailing event.

Agriculture also plays a major role in diet, from locally grown sugar beets and potatoes to buckwheat and rye. That means you'll find many breads and porridges, to which milk or a fruit sauce is added, a Danish influence.

The *Lüneburger Heidekartoffeln* are firm boiling potatoes with pale, smooth skin and yellow flesh, grown in Lower Saxony. Many local restaurants feature these potatoes in their menus. Germany's first "potato hotel," where tubers reign in décor and menus, is the Kartoffel Hotel Lüneburger Heide (a spa resort).

Spring restaurant menus showcase much more white than green asparagus. A classic entrée is fresh asparagus spears and new potatoes with hollandaise sauce.

Sprat, a popular type of herring, harvested in Kiel, a city that loves sailing.

A creamy potato soup arrives with strips of smoked salmon and carrots. Pea soup is a popular way to ease a nip in the air on cool days. Tasty entrées include pork medallions with fresh mushrooms, served over penne pasta, and a stew of scampi, crab, and tomato that is served with spaghetti.

Cooks also take cues from Russia and Poland, sometimes using *Schmand*—sweet and sour creams— to make smooth and rich soups and gravies. Dishes that combine fruits, vegetables, and meats also are common, as are fruit soups that double as light entrées. Popular and unique mixes include *Birnen, Bohnen, und Speck* (pears, green beans, and bacon), *Grünkohl und Pinkel* (kale and sausage), and *Snuten und Poten* (pig's snout and sauerkraut), a Hamburg favorite.

The love of seafood extends to Hamburg, where the weekly harborside fish market is in full swing by 6 AM on Sundays. You know you're heading in the right direction when you encounter dozens of people with bags of fresh fish, flowers, fruits, and vegetables. Inside the sturdy, brick Fish Auction House, old Blues Brothers music might blare and dozens are having their first beer of the day. At the market's east end, clothing and souvenirs are sold. At the west end, small trees, other plants, and hanging baskets of flowers are grouped together in colorful displays.

And in the middle, much of the hawking of fruits and veggies grows intense. Closest to the waterfront are the fresh fish vendors and those who sell herring sandwiches. Also for sale are smoked fillets, eel, herring, and variety packs of raw fish; the latter option increases as morning draws closer to noon than dawn. Some vendors make the crowd laugh. Others mumble or roar. Still others slap together four- to six-piece fish assortments, only to return each to its original place if a hard sell doesn't work. It makes for fine food theater, and sometimes, quick fish sales.

Also in Hamburg is a museum devoted to spices, on the third floor of an old warehouse, above a shop that sells Persian rugs. Burlap sacks are filled with raw spices, and other displays feature antique spice holders and processing equipment. Spice sales and samplings also occur. One lesson to be learned here: Nutmeg, cloves, cinnamon, mace, and pepper were the first five spices brought to Germany by the Dutch East Indies Company during their first trips from the Far East.

For other evidence of culinary diversity, take an eat-the-world tour. The emphasis is on ethnicity, and that might mean sampling *Nata,* a sweet pudding with Portuguese roots, or eating tofu, noodles, and veggies in a tomato-marine sauce at an organic restaurant. The five-stop tour through less-touristy areas is meant to demonstrate the food world beyond what is predictable in Germany. That said, samples might also include pan fish and sliced potatoes in a mustard sauce—or marzipan in the shape of a naked woman, a tribute to the prostitutes who do business near racy St. Pauli Street.

Much quieter is the Brauhaus Johannes Albrecht, which overlooks a quiet canal far inland. Quell a light appetite with German tapas—saucy meatballs, sausage salad, sausages on sauerkraut, and fried potatoes—while quenching your thirst with a chilled beer.

Or, take a city ferry to Hamburg's Elbterrassen neighborhood near the floating ships museum, and linger at an outdoor cafe with a baked potato blanketed with sour cream and many tiny North Sea shrimp, which are shipped to Morocco and Algeria for cleaning and deshelling, then sent back to Germany for consumption.

Holsteiner Karpfen, a mirror carp, was the first fish in this area to gain PGI status. The fish's firm, white meat is low in fat content, and the species has been significant in Schleswig-Holstein since pond farming began there in 1196. It is the most northern part of Germany where carp are harvested.

The region's other geographically distinct products include *Ammerländer Schinken* and *Ammerländer Knochenschinken,* dry-cured, spiced and smoked ham, with or without a bone, made with meat from a specific breed of pig since the 18th century. The pork is rubbed with a mix of sea salt, brown sugar, and sometimes a spice blend of juniper, pepper, and allspice. Both *Ammerländer Dielenrauchschinken* and *Ammerländer Katenschinken* refer to a notable plank-smoked ham from the same area.

Holsteiner Katenschinken, Holsteiner Schinken, Holsteiner Katenrauchschinken, and *Holsteiner Knochenschinken* describe a bone-in ham, salted by hand, dry-cured for up to eight weeks and slowly cold-smoked over beechwood. The Schleswig-Holstein production process takes at least four months. The meat is red and slightly marbled, smoky in taste, and with a fat that tastes mildly nutty. The ham is sold whole or in slices. The oldest reference to it is from 1608; the region's ham and bacon were traded for West Indies sugar and rum in the 18th century. At restaurants, the ham is often served with locally grown asparagus. Some of the traditional ham smokehouses are open to tourists.

Other regionally significant meats are *Lüneburger Heidschnucke,* a lean and gamey meat from a heritage breed of sheep raised near Lüneburg since 1848, and *Diepholzer Moorschnucke,* a tender and gamey meat from a heritage

Artifacts span several centuries at Spicy's Gewürzmuseum (spice museum), Hamburg.

breed of moorland sheep that has come close to extinction. Only 40 of the animals were documented in 1974.

Two brews in the region gain PGI status. *Bremer Bier* refers to an assortment of beer produced in a specific manner for about 800 years. At least eight types, *Schankbier* (draft beer) to *Bockbier* (bock beer), are sold. The beer has been in demand throughout northern Europe since the 13th century. Brauerei Beck & Co., a key producer in the late 1800s, was the first German brewery to add ice-making equipment, so beer could cool evenly all year. Bremen breweries are Germany's top beer exporters.

The other PGI is for *Dortmunder Bier,* a trio of beer types—pilsner, low-alcohol, and alt—produced in a specific manner for centuries in Dortmund. A 1904 court judgment confirmed these products are geographically significant.

Among northern Germany's best-known regional products is *Lübecker Marzipan,* a confection made from fresh ground almonds, sugar, and spices. The treat became a specialty in the 19th century, and the seventh-generation Niederegger company, which makes 50 tons of marzipan daily, is home to a free museum that explains the product's history. Work for Christmas orders begins in August. There are 500 employees, plus 250 seasonal workers, and about 300 products, with exports to 35 countries. The marzipan products started as a medicine, not a candy, and only a pharmacist could own or prescribe it. It was then considered an aphrodisiac and also added to medications to help make them taste better. Today's marzipan products have a six- to nine-month shelf life and hand-carved marzipan treats are customary. Marzipan that is shaped like a pig is a symbol of good luck.

Other regionally significant sweet treats include *Salzwedeler Baumkuchen,* a round, many-layered cake whose cut pieces resemble tree rings. The dessert can be as big as 3 feet tall, 15 inches wide, and weigh up to 11 pounds. It is served on birthdays and holidays, but many of the cakes also are exported. The recipe dates back to 1807, as written by a local baker. Ingredients and production are costly and have not changed since the cake's creation. The cake is baked on an open fire, and dough is applied with a ladle, one layer at a time, on a rotating spit. Coatings range from fondant icing to frostings of dark chocolate, white chocolate, or milk chocolate.

Also distinct in the area is *Bremer Klaben,* a rich, yeast-based cake with high fruit content. The dough-to-fruit ratio is 1-to-1, and the product has been noted as a regional specialty since 1593. The cake is similar to *Stollen* but is bigger, has more fruit, and has a shiny, egg-white glaze. Sometimes rum

Marzipan carving and decorating are ongoing at the free Niederegger Museum, Lübeck.

or rose oil is added. Like *Stollen,* it is standard regional fare during the Christmas season, but the cake also was popular with sailors because it did not spoil easily.

German chocolate cake is not from Germany, despite its name. The popular American dessert with sugary coconut frosting was created by a Texan in 1957. "German" refers to a sweet baking chocolate invented by Samuel German, an American baker. And although Americans consider cake a typical and acceptable dessert, Germans are more likely to have their slice of cake with coffee between meals.

No matter what you eat or where you roam in Germany, you can't go wrong by complimenting the cook, butcher, or baker by saying *das war gut* (that was good) or *das war lecker* (that was delicious) after a meal or nibble.

Tastes of Germany

Dip into this mix of classic and nouveau recipes to better understand the range of culinary delights that defines Germany. Notice how some chefs—as is the case worldwide—incorporate elements of other cultures into their cooking.

Street food to Michelin-rated cuisine is represented in this selective collection of appetizers to desserts that can be replicated in your own kitchen. Some entrées require days of planning because of lengthy (but worthwhile!) marinating time.

Note that chefs tend to add a bouquet garni of herbs and spices to marinades and later remove and discard these seasonings. This is easy to do because herbs and spices are held together with string or tied inside a small pouch of cheesecloth.

Most ingredients are easy to obtain at grocery or gourmet specialty stores, or consult *Resources*, p. 79, for mail-order sources. Local substitutes for foreign ingredients are also noted.

BEVERAGE

Glühwein

Mulled wine. Serves 4.

The opening of *Christkindlmarkts* in late November is a traditional and popular prelude to the celebration of Christmas in Germany. The drinking of steamy *Glühwein* with friends is a standard part of these outdoor gatherings, from small towns to metropolitan areas.

This recipe comes from the German National Tourism Office.

4½ CUPS DRY RED WINE

1 LEMON, SLICED

2 CINNAMON STICKS

3 CLOVES

[Glühwein, *continued*]

> 3 TABLESPOONS SUGAR
>
> CARDAMOM, TO TASTE

Heat the red wine. Add lemon slices to the hot wine. Add remaining ingredients and heat about 5 minutes. Remove from heat, cover, and allow to infuse for 1 hour. Reheat and pass through a sieve before serving.

APPETIZERS

Obatzda mit Birnen und Croûtons

Obatzda *with pears and croutons*. Serves 4–6.

Obatzda is a traditional soft-cheese spread that is slathered onto radishes, bread, rolls, or fat pretzels in Bavaria. Some versions stir a splash of beer into the snack that is eaten while drinking beer. This recipe from chef Alfons Schuhbeck of Munich, who operates Schuhbecks Kochschule, entices with pears and pear brandy.

> *Croutons*
>
> 2 SLICES WHITE BREAD
>
> 3 TABLESPOONS BUTTER
>
> 2 TABLESPOONS OIL
>
> Obatzda *with pear*
>
> ½ RIPE, FIRM PEAR
>
> 4 GREEN ONIONS
>
> 8 OUNCES RIPE CAMEMBERT
>
> 8 OUNCES CREAM CHEESE
>
> 2–3 TABLESPOONS CREAM
>
> 2 TABLESPOONS PEAR BRANDY
>
> SALT, TO TASTE
>
> PINCH OF CAYENNE PEPPER
>
> PINCH OF GROUND CARAWAY SEEDS
>
> BROWN BUTTER*

Remove crust from bread. Slice bread into the smallest possible cubes. (The chef notes this is easier if the bread slices are somewhat frozen.)
Heat butter and oil in a skillet. Brown the bread cubes over medium heat until light brown. Drain on a paper towel.

Bring Camembert and cream cheeses to room temperature. Peel and core pear, then dice finely. Cut green onions into thin slices. Cut room-temperature Camembert into small pieces and mix in a bowl with cream cheese, cream, and pear brandy until creamy. Fold in diced pear and green onions. Season with salt, cayenne pepper, caraway seeds, and brown butter. To serve, fill a serving dish with the *Obatzda* and sprinkle croutons on top.

*Brown butter is butter that is cooked just beyond melting. When cooled, add it to the *Obatzda* as desired, for extra flavor.

Tartar von der Buhlbach-Forelle mit Meerrettich, Apfelgelee

Buhlbach trout tartare with horseradish, apple gelée. Serves 6.

In the Black Forest's Baiersbronn area are nine villages with a total population of 16,000. At last count, three restaurants there had accumulated an amazing seven Michelin stars.

The award winners include the family-owned Hotel Sackmann, which markets itself as a Black Forest wellness hotel that provides a refined combination of relaxation and good food in a spectacular setting. The gracious Jörg Sackmann, who represents the third generation of owners, is generous with his recipes, including this light and refreshing first course featuring trout from Lake Buhlbach. Local trout may be substituted.

Trout and marinade

2 BUHLBACH TROUT FILLETS

⅓ CUP LEMON BALM, WITH STEMS

SEA SALT, TO TASTE

⅛ CUP MUSCOVADO SUGAR (OR DARK BROWN SUGAR)

1 TEASPOON CRUSHED PEPPERCORNS

1 TEASPOON CRUSHED CORIANDER SEEDS

1 TABLESPOON OLIVE OIL

1½ OUNCES VODKA

SPLASH OF LEMON JUICE

Tartare mixture

½ CUP PEELED AND CUBED GRANNY SMITH APPLES

½ CUP PEELED, SEEDED, AND CUBED CUCUMBERS

1 TABLESPOON FINELY CHOPPED LEMON BALM

1 TABLESPOON OLIVE OIL

2 SHALLOTS, FINELY CHOPPED

[Tartar von der Buhlbach-Forelle mit Meerrettich, Apfelgelee, *continued*]

Horseradish cream

½ CUP SOUR CREAM

1 TEASPOON FRESHLY GRATED HORSERADISH

PINCH CAYENNE PEPPER

SALT, TO TASTE

LEMON JUICE, TO TASTE

Apple gelée

4 GRANNY SMITH APPLES

1 LEMON

5 SHEETS GELATIN

SALT, TO TASTE

PINCH SUGAR

PINCH CAYENNE PEPPER

Place the fillets with the skin side down in a shallow pan. Cut the lemon balm coarsely and mix well with the remaining marinade ingredients. Spread the mixture evenly over the fillets, cover with foil, and marinate in the refrigerator. After about 6 hours, turn the fillets and marinate for another 6 hours. Remove and discard the skin from the marinated trout. Cut the fish into small cubes.

Combine the tartare ingredients. Add the cubed fish.

Combine the horseradish cream ingredients.

For the apple gelée, juice the apples, add lemon juice to taste. Heat the juice briefly and add the softened sheets of gelatin. Season with salt, sugar, and cayenne pepper. Pour the mixture into a form to set. Cut the gelatin into strips, roughly 1" × 4". To serve, place apple gelée strips in the middle of the plate. Arrange the tartare, using a food ring, and add a dollop of horseradish cream.

Handkäse mit Musik

Hand cheese with music. Serves many.

This regional Hessen specialty starts with a pungent yellow cheese that traditionally was made by hand. Today, Harzer and Mainzer brands of the cheese are sold in ethnic food stores. The cheese–onion combo is an acquired taste; "with music" refers to the potential for the bread spread to give diners intestinal gas.

This recipe is from Andreas Fritsche, executive chef at the elegant Radisson Blu Schwarzer Bock Hotel, Wiesbaden, which was established in 1486 as a traditional bathhouse. The thermal spa remains accessible to hotel guests. Capricorne, the hotel's fine dining restaurant, mixes regional and international specialties.

7 OUNCES (4 PIECES) HAND CHEESE

½ CUP FINELY CHOPPED ONION

½ CUP APPLE WINE VINEGAR*

⅓ CUP VEGETABLE OIL

2 TABLESPOONS CARAWAY SEEDS†

SALT AND FRESH PEPPER, TO TASTE

BROWN BREAD††

BUTTER

Prepare a marinade from all the ingredients and pour it over the hand cheese. Let it sit in the refrigerator in a covered container for 12 hours.

Serve the hand cheese arranged on a plate with marinade sprinkled over it lightly, decorated as desired, and with fresh bread and butter.

*Apple cider vinegar is an adequate substitute.

†Some restaurants serve caraway separately instead of mixing it into the marinade.

††Germans prefer *Graubrot,* which is made from several different flours.

SALADS

Spargelfest Salat

Grilled asparagus and beet salad with honey mustard. Serves 4.

German Foods North America, LLC, promotes the global trade of Germany's food products and paves the way for average consumers to experiment in their kitchens through www.germanfoods.org, which publishes dozens of traditional and contemporary recipes. This one is representative of the country's fresh flavors and products. The ingredient list encourages the use of German products, but local brands may be substituted.

20 YOUNG, PENCIL-THIN ASPARAGUS SPEARS, WASHED AND TRIMMED

2 TABLESPOONS OLIVE OIL

2 TABLESPOONS GERMAN VINEGAR

2 TEASPOONS GERMAN HONEY

2 TEASPOONS GERMAN SWEET MUSTARD

2 TABLESPOONS FRESH LEMON JUICE

3 TABLESPOONS MINCED SHALLOTS

SALT AND PEPPER, TO TASTE

¾ CUP OLIVE OIL

[Spargelfest Salat, *continued*]

6 CUPS EUROPEAN SALAD MIX, WASHED AND TRIMMED

19-OUNCE JAR GERMAN RED BEET BALLS, DRAINED

4 OUNCES SLICED, PAPER-THIN BLACK FOREST–STYLE HAM OR
GERMAN PROSCIUTTO

6 OUNCES CRUMBLED GERMAN *CAMBOZOLA* CHEESE, DIVIDED*

⅓ CUP TOASTED PINE NUTS

4 SLICES TOASTED GERMAN BREAD†

2 TABLESPOONS BUTTER

Preheat oven to 400°F. Cover baking sheet with parchment paper, line asparagus on
paper, and brush with olive oil. Roast in oven for 6 minutes.

Combine vinegar, honey, mustard, lemon juice, shallots, salt, and pepper in a small
bowl. Slowly whisk in olive oil to blend.

Line four salad plates with European salad mix, divide beets among salads,
attractively roll and arrange ham/prosciutto over salads, and top each with five
spears of grilled asparagus. Sprinkle salads with 2 ounces of *Cambozola* and pine
nuts. Stir vinaigrette and adjust seasoning if desired; drizzle over salads.

Butter toasted bread; cut each slice diagonally in half twice to form four triangles;
sprinkle with remaining 4 ounces *Cambozola* and place in hot oven, just to soften
and warm cheese. Place four triangles attractively around each salad.

*Cambozola is a type of gourmet blue-veined cheese.

†Whole rye, *Fitnessbrot,* sunflower seed, or pumpernickel is recommended.

Deutsch-Stil Heringssalat

German-style herring salad. Serves 4.

Chef Ludger Szmania is a Düsseldorf native who opened the restaurant Szmania's in
Seattle in 1999. He uses pickled herring in this recipe for German Foods North
America and www.germanfoods.org. Serve this salad with German pumpernickel or
sunflower bread.

1 CAN (12–16 OUNCES) PICKLED HERRING

½ CUP SLICED GERMAN DILL PICKLES, CUT INTO STRIPS OF 1½ × ¼ INCHES

½ MEDIUM GRANNY SMITH APPLE, DICED

½ CUP SOUR CREAM

SALT AND PEPPER, TO TASTE

1 TABLESPOON FRESH CHOPPED PARSLEY

2 CUPS MESCLUN SALAD MIX

2 PLUM TOMATOES, SLICED IN WEDGES

Drain herring and remove pickling spices. Pat with a paper towel to dry as much as possible and place in bowl. Add pickle, apple, sour cream, and parsley. Stir gently with a rubber spatula. Season with salt and pepper. Divide mesclun mix and sliced tomatoes among four plates. Divide herring salad among plates, on top of the greens.

Kartoffelsalat

Potato salad. Serves 4–6.

Chefs at Mader's Restaurant in Milwaukee, voted North America's most famous German restaurant, have prepared potato salad the same way for more than 60 years. Restaurant manager Mary Niland shares the recipe, which was written by the late Katie Mader.

> 1 QUART POTATOES (4–5 MEDIUM)
>
> ¼ POUND BACON, DICED
>
> ½ CUP ONION
>
> ¼ CUP SUGAR
>
> 1 TEASPOON SALT
>
> 2 TABLESPOONS FLOUR
>
> ½ CUP VINEGAR
>
> ½ CUP WATER
>
> FRESH PARSLEY, FINELY MINCED

Cook potatoes, without peeling, only until tender. Drain and peel while still warm. Slice and set aside.

Cook bacon until crisp, then drain on unglazed paper. Pour off all but 2 tablespoons of bacon fat. Add onion to bacon fat and cook and stir until transparent, not brown. Add sugar, salt and flour, blending thoroughly. Add vinegar and water, then cook and stir until smooth and thickened. Add potato slices and bacon bits, folding ingredients together carefully to avoid breaking the potato slices. Allow to stand in a warm place, so potatoes will absorb the flavor of the dressing. Transfer to a warm serving dish. Garnish with parsley.

SOUPS

Kartoffelsuppe

Potato soup. Serves 4.

The playwright Johann Wolfgang von Goethe frequented the historic Auerbachs Keller while he was a student in Leipzig, and he made the historic cellar restaurant (located below a shopping arcade) a setting for his tragic play *Faust I*. Sculptures

[Kartoffelsuppe, *continued*]

and murals from this story enrich the décor of Auerbachs Keller. The restaurant's chefs share this simple but delicious soup recipe.

⅛ CUP LARD

½ CUP SLICED ONION

½ CUP SLICED LEEK

⅛ CUP FLOUR

2½ CUPS CHICKEN BROTH

½ POUND POTATOES (2 MEDIUM), PEELED AND THINLY SLICED

1 TEASPOON MARJORAM

PINCH NUTMEG

SALT AND PEPPER, TO TASTE

CROUTONS

Melt lard in saucepan, then sweat onions and leeks. Dust mixture with flour and continue to sweat until translucent. Add broth, potatoes, and seasonings; cover and bring to a boil. Simmer until potatoes are soft. Serve with croutons.

Sauerkrautsuppe
Sauerkraut soup. Serves 4.

Food writer and home economist Roz Denny of England shares this hearty recipe in her book *Modern German Cooking* and with German Foods North America, an agency in Washington, DC, that promotes the use of German food products. The addition of your choice of smoked sausage could qualify this as a main meal. Serve with German whole-grain rye bread.

10-OUNCE JAR GERMAN SAUERKRAUT

1 ONION, CHOPPED

1 LARGE GARLIC CLOVE, CRUSHED

4¼ CUPS COLD WATER

9 OUNCES *SPECK* OR BACON, CHOPPED

½ TEASPOON GROUND PAPRIKA

2 TEASPOONS CHOPPED FRESH DILL

4½ OUNCES SMOKED SAUSAGE, SLICED OR CHOPPED

5 OUNCES SOUR CREAM

SEA SALT AND FRESHLY GROUND BLACK PEPPER, TO TASTE

Rinse sauerkraut in cold water and drain. Place sauerkraut, onion, garlic, and cold water in a large saucepan. Bring to a boil, then simmer for 15 minutes. Meanwhile, fry bacon in a deep frying pan until the fat starts to run. Stir in the paprika and stir into the sauerkraut mixture. Return to a gentle simmer for another 15 minutes, then add the dill and sausage of your choice. Stir in the cream, check the seasoning, and reheat until just to the point of boiling.

Serbska Kwasna Poliwka

Sorbian wedding soup. Serves 6–8.

In a Saxony valley along the Spree River is the steep and medieval-looking community of Bautzen, where much of Germany's prepared mustard is made. A mustard museum is one of the compact city's popular tourist attractions.

About 5 percent of the city's population is Sorbian, and they work hard to preserve their way of life and history, which dates back to 1002. The Sorbs have their own language, street signs, clothing style, and cultural traditions.

Veronika Mahling welcomes guests to Restaurant Wjelbik, where diners are treated to a traditional Sorbian meal, delivered with song by staff wearing traditional Sorbian attire. The specific costume that a Sorbian woman wears depends upon her age and marital status.

Local resident and tour guide Madlena Kowar shares a recipe for the soup that is a part of the special meal. Instructions have survived many generations and come from "an old Sorbian book, so it's original. Today some people add pasta and other vegetables."

Broth

1 CARROT

½ CELERIAC

1 ONION

1 TABLESPOON LARD

1 CUP CAULIFLOWER, IN SMALL PIECES

4 CUPS MEAT BROTH

Meatballs

7 OUNCES GROUND LIVER (LIVERWURST)

1 EGG

½ CUP BREAD CRUMBS

PINCH NUTMEG

SALT AND PEPPER, TO TASTE

[Serbska Kwasna Poliwka, *continued*]

Eggs

4 EGGS

1 CUP COLD MILK

PINCH NUTMEG

SALT, TO TASTE

Peel and cut carrot, celeriac, and onion into small pieces. Melt lard, add cut vegetables, cook until softened, add a small amount of water, cover, and simmer until tender. In a separate pan, add 1 cup water to cauliflower pieces, heat, cover and simmer until tender. Place the cooked vegetables, undrained, into the meat broth. Simmer. To make meatballs, combine liverwurst and egg. Blend dry ingredients and add to meat mixture. Refrigerate for one hour, then form small balls (½") and add to the simmering broth. Heat until the meatballs swim to the top. While bringing a pot of water to a boil, mix eggs, milk, nutmeg, and salt. Pour into a zipper-style plastic bag, close, and place in boiling water. When firm, remove. Cut egg mixture into small pieces and add to the soup shortly before serving.

Rote Bete Suppe mit Meerrettich und Jakobsmuschel

Beet soup with horseradish and scallops. Serves 6–8.

When chef Florian Neumann of the Maritim Hotel in Berlin was a mere 20 years old, he earned a gold award in Worldskills competition sponsored by the World Association of Chefs Societies. The German-based Maritim lodging group is family-owned, and the chef shares his country's love for beets through this beautiful recipe.

1 CUP PEELED AND CHOPPED BEETS, RAW OR PRECOOKED

1 SHALLOT, PEELED AND CHOPPED

3 TO 4 CUPS BEEF OR CHICKEN BROTH

BOUQUET GARNI OF MUSTARD SEED, BAY LEAF, ALLSPICE, AND

(IF DESIRED) CLOVES

1 FRESH SEA SCALLOP PER SERVING

1½ TABLESPOONS BUTTER

1 TEASPOON FRESHLY GRATED HORSERADISH

SALT, PEPPER, SUGAR, AND VINEGAR, TO TASTE

½ CUP CREAM OR CRÈME FRAÎCHE

Add beets, shallot, broth, and bouquet garni to saucepan. Simmer, at least until vegetables soften, then add horseradish and purée. Add salt, pepper, sugar, and vinegar to taste. While purée cools slightly, sauté scallops in butter until opaque. Add cream or crème fraîche to purée. Place one scallop in each soup bowl. Add purée.

Schwarz Kirschsuppe

Black cherry soup. Serves 4.

This classic recipe comes from Marcel Biró, a native of East Germany and personal chef to former German Chancellor Helmut Kohl. The master chef in 1999 moved to Wisconsin, where he operated a cooking school and published award-winning cookbooks. In 2012, he became Vice President of Hospitality at Helms College in Augusta, Georgia, which operates Edgar's Grill on campus.

Biró: European-Inspired Cuisine (Gibbs Smith, 2005) contains his adaptations of Old World recipes that have stood the test of time. Marcel recommends this one for Valentine's Day. "Cherries have long been reputed to be an aphrodisiac," he suggests, "and the seductive flavor and texture and vibrant color of this soup make it the ideal prelude to any romantic meal. I especially like it served before pork or filet mignon."

1½ POUNDS RIPE BLACK CHERRIES, UNPITTED, DIVIDED*

⅔ CUP FRUITY WHITE WINE

1 CINNAMON STICK

⅔ CUP WATER

2 TABLESPOONS SUGAR†

GRATED PEEL AND JUICE OF 1 LEMON

1¼ CUPS GERMAN DOUBLE CREAM OR CRÈME FRAÎCHE, DIVIDED††

2 TABLESPOONS ASBACH URALT OR OTHER BRANDY

Remove the stems and pits from the cherries but do not discard. Place one-half of the pits in a clean kitchen towel or freezer bag and crush them with a mallet. Keep the other half of the pits intact.

In a large saucepan, combine the crushed pits, whole pits, stems, wine, cinnamon, water, sugar, lemon peel, and lemon juice. Bring to a boil over medium heat, then cover and simmer for 10 minutes.

Remove from heat and strain the liquid through a fine-mesh sieve. Return the liquid to the pan. Stir in 1 cup of the double cream or crème fraîche and all but one-quarter of the cherries. Simmer over medium-low heat for 5 minutes, whisking occasionally.

In a food processor or blender, purée the cherry mixture until smooth. Refrigerate until cool, and then whisk in the Asbach Uralt. Chill until ready to serve.

Presentation: Because of the vibrant color, serve soup in a plain white bowl or a chilled, clear glass bowl or cup. Drizzle the remaining ¼ cup of the cream or crème fraîche atop the soup and garnish with the remaining cherries.

*Sour cherries or a jar of ARO Schattenmorellen cherries may be substituted.

†German cherry syrup, to taste, may be substituted.

††German double cream has a higher fat content than the whipping cream available in the United States. Crème fraîche is a suitable substitute.

Main Dishes

Bäckeoffe

Meat and vegetable stew. Serves 6.

Chef Dieter Jindra of Restaurant Gugelhof, located in a former East Germany neighborhood of Berlin, shares his version of a traditional stew of marinated meats that are braised with root vegetables in a clay pot and covered with a layer of bread dough. The recipe name means "baker's oven," and the stew is traditional in Alsace, France, which borders southwestern Germany.

Restaurant Gugelhof is known for its hearty meals, rustic setting, and friendly service in a trendy restaurant area (Kollwitzplatz). Former German Chancellor Schröder and former U.S. President Clinton ate dinner there in 2000.

8 OUNCES BEEF*

8 OUNCES LAMB*

8 OUNCES PORK*

1 CARROT

1 STALK CELERY

1 ONION

4 WHOLE CLOVES

1 BAY LEAF

1 GARLIC CLOVE, PEELED

4¼ CUPS SEMI-DRY WHITE WINE, PREFERABLY ALSATIAN RIESLING†

2 POUNDS POTATOES (ABOUT 6), PEELED AND SLICED

1 CUP SLICED ONION

SALT AND PEPPER, TO TASTE

ALL INGREDIENTS FOR YEAST DOUGH††

Dice the meat into pieces about ½" long. Peel the carrot and slice it and the celery into thick pieces. Remove onion skin, then stick cloves into the onion.

Put the meat, carrot, celery, whole onion with cloves, bay leaf, and garlic into a bowl. Add white wine. Cover and refrigerate overnight.

The next day, preheat oven to 350°F. Separate marinade from the meats and chopped vegetables, and set aside. Remove and discard the garlic, bay leaf, and onion with cloves.

Peel potatoes and cut into slices. Fill a clay pot with layers of ingredients that are seasoned, to taste, with salt and pepper. Begin with one-half of the potato slices, then one-half of the onion slices, then all of the meat (with chopped, marinated vegetables). Add remaining onion slices and finish with the remaining potato slices. Pour the reserved wine marinade over all layers. Close the clay pot with a tight lid and place it in the oven for 2½–3 hours.

Prepare enough yeast dough to roll out and cover the top of the clay pot. Carefully replace the pot lid with the dough. Bake another 15–20 minutes, until golden brown.

*Although meat cuts are not specified, boneless sirloin tip steak works fine for the beef, as does stew meat for the lamb and boneless center cut loin chops for the pork.

†Wollersheim Winery's Prairie Fumé is an adequate substitute for Alsatian Riesling.

††The dough for three or four frozen bread rolls, thawed, or one-half of a Pillsbury French bread loaf, is an easy substitute for made-from-scratch yeast dough.

Odenwälder Mostbraten

Marinated pot roast. Serves 4–6.

Philipp Spengel, sixth-generation owner (with wife Anne) of Zum Roten Ochsen (Red Ox Inn), Heidelberg, shares the makings for a meal of pure comfort food. Especially delectable is the rich gravy. Days of marinating make the meat tender and flavorful.

Zum Roten Ochsen is a much-loved casual restaurant near Karlsplatz and a perennial favorite of college students. The chef-owners have traditionally lived above the restaurant.

> 1 ONION
>
> 1 CARROT
>
> ½ LEEK
>
> ½ CELERIAC
>
> 2 POUNDS BONELESS SHOULDER ROAST
>
> BOUQUET GARNI OF JUNIPER BERRIES, MUSTARD SEED, AND PEPPERCORNS
>
> (ALL COARSELY CRUSHED); BAY LEAF, WHOLE CLOVES
>
> 1 CUP STRONG RED WINE
>
> 1 CUP WATER
>
> ½ CUP APPLE WINE*
>
> VEGETABLE OIL
>
> SALT AND PEPPER, TO TASTE
>
> 2 TABLESPOONS TOMATO PASTE
>
> CORNSTARCH, AS NEEDED

Coarsely chop the onion, carrot, leek, and celeriac. Place these vegetables and the bouquet garni with the beef in a nonmetallic container that can be covered. Mix wine, water, and apple wine. Pour over meat, vegetables, and spice mix. Cover. For the best results, marinate for 2–4 days.

Preheat oven to 350°F. Drain and reserve marinade. Discard bouquet garni. Heat oil in roasting pan.

[Odenwälder Mostbraten, *continued*]

Remove meat, dry it, season with salt and pepper and brown quickly in a roasting pan. Remove. Sweat the vegetables (sauté lightly, without browning), add tomato paste, then quench with the marinade. Put the meat back in the pot, cover tightly, and place in oven for 1½–2 hours.

When the meat is done (test for tenderness with a fork), remove it from the pan and keep warm. Place pan on stovetop; let the sauce cook and reduce. If needed, thicken with cornstarch and adjust flavor. The sauce should taste slightly sour.

Serve with potato or flour dumplings and a mix of apples and red cabbage (see Side Dishes, p. 59).

*Apple cider vinegar is an adequate substitute.

Schweinefilet mit Apfelwein, Buntem Gemüsen, und Kartoffeln

Pork fillet with apple wine, colorful vegetables, and potatoes. Serves 4.

Executive Chef Andreas Fritsche of the Radisson Blu Schwarzer Bock Hotel, Wiesbaden, shares this much-loved regional specialty. The hotel's architectural showpiece is the Ingelheimer Zimmer, an historic ballroom with 16th-century woodcarvings.

2¼ POUNDS PORK FILLET

2 TABLESPOONS OIL

SALT AND PEPPER, TO TASTE

1 POUND SMALL POTATOES, WITH SKINS

4 CUPS PEELED AND CUBED ROOT VEGETABLES (A MIX, FOR EXAMPLE,

    OF CARROTS, CELERIAC, KOHLRABI, AND PARSNIPS)

1¼ CUPS APPLE WINE*

2 CUPS VEAL STOCK

1 SPRIG ROSEMARY

1 SPRIG THYME

Preheat oven to 325°F. Remove tendons and fat from the pork fillet. Heat oil in roaster pan, season pork with salt and pepper, then brown it on all sides. Remove the meat and set aside. In the same pan, fry the potatoes about 10 minutes on a low flame. Add the cubed vegetables and fry for a short time. Put the pork fillet on top of the vegetables and quench with apple wine and veal stock.

Bring to a boil, add the herbs, and season with additional salt and pepper. Cover and roast in the oven for about 20 minutes.

To serve, slice the pork fillet into medallions and arrange in the center of a plate. Distribute the vegetables and potatoes around the meat. Add a little of the unthickened sauce; garnish as desired.

*Use a German *Apfelwein* (apple wine) for the most authentic results.

Wiener Schnitzel
Breaded veal cutlet. Serves 4.

There are many variations of this German classic; this standard version comes from chef-owner Herbert Beltle of Aigner Gendarmenmarkt, a charming and linen-clad Berlin restaurant that serves a mix of Austrian and German cuisine. The restaurant name comes from a once-famous Viennese café that closed in the 1980s.

2 POUNDS VEAL

5 EGGS

SALT AND PEPPER, TO TASTE

1 CUP FLOUR

4 CUPS FINELY GROUND BREAD CRUMBS

VEGETABLE OIL

CRANBERRY MARMALADE (OPTIONAL)

Cleanly pare the veal, freeing it from fat and tendons. Then cut it into four same-sized pieces. Place each piece between plastic wrap and flatten it carefully with a meat hammer, until thin. Be careful not to hammer holes into the meat.

Crack the eggs into a wide bowl and beat coarsely with a fork.

Salt and pepper the meat, then turn both sides in the flour, then eggs, then bread crumbs. Cook the breaded schnitzel immediately in hot oil. Be careful that the oil is neither too hot nor too cold. Keep the *Schnitzel* in constant movement in the pan. This allows the breading to release from the meat so the *Schnitzel* can puff up nicely. If desired, serve with cranberry marmalade.

Rouladen
Rolls of stuffed beef. Serves 2–3.

Michelle Clasen-Werry of Clasen's European Bakery, Middleton, Wisconsin, shares her great-grandmother's Rhineland interpretation of a classic and popular German entrée. Americanized versions of the recipe typically contain too much bacon, or cooks don't brown the beef long enough, which results in a sauce that doesn't reach its lusciously rich potential.

6 SLICES ROUND STEAK, ¼-INCH THICK (1½–2 POUNDS)

SALT AND PEPPER, TO TASTE

10 OUNCES GROUND PORK

12 PEARL ONIONS

6 SMALL DILL PICKLES, CHOPPED

1 BUNCH ITALIAN PARSLEY, CHOPPED

FLOUR (FOR COATING)

[Rouladen, *continued*]

    4 TABLESPOONS CANOLA OIL

    3 SMALL ONIONS, QUARTERED

    1 CUP BEEF BROTH

    1 CUP WATER

    1 CUP RED WINE

    2 TABLESPOONS TOMATO PASTE

Season round steak with salt and pepper. Distribute and spread the ground pork over each slice of the meat. Sprinkle with pearl onions, chopped pickles and parsley. Roll each topped beef slice into a tight roll. Tie each roll with kitchen twine, to resemble a nice log. Salt, pepper, and dust each roll with flour.
Heat oil on medium high in frying pan. Sear each meat roll in the hot pan, turning over when sides are browned very well. It is important to sear the meat a deep brown; this will give the gravy a better flavor.
Add the onion quarters and cook a few minutes, reducing the heat to medium low. Add beef broth and water. Bring to a boil, reduce heat, cover and simmer about 90 minutes. Turn the meat occasionally while it simmers.
Remove the meat rolls and set aside. Bring pan liquid to a boil, and reduce to one-half the original quantity. Mix red wine with tomato paste and add to the pan liquid. Bring to a boil, and reduce for about 10 minutes to thicken the sauce. Season to taste with additional salt and pepper. Remove string from each meat roll and add back to the sauce. Heat a few minutes and serve with *Spätzle* or potatoes.

Pflanzerl

Bavarian burgers. Serves 4–6.
Chef Alfons Schuhbeck of Munich earned his Michelin star in 1983, three years after taking over his parents' restaurant in Germany. The Gault Millau, a French gourmet restaurant guide, in 1989 chose him as Chef of the Year. Since 2003, Schuhbeck has operated several culinary enterprises, including Schuhbecks Kochschule in Munich, through which he seeks to stimulate the palate in nontraditional ways, especially through the innovative use of spices.
These seasoned meat patties are prepared like the American hamburger, but the taste profile is more complex. These burgers contain pork, so be sure to serve them well-done.

    3 SLICES WHITE BREAD

    ½ CUP MILK

    ½ ONION, DICED

    1 TABLESPOON OIL

2 EGGS

2 TEASPOONS HOT MUSTARD

SALT, TO TASTE

FRESHLY GROUND PEPPER, TO TASTE

PINCH OF FRESHLY GRATED NUTMEG

PINCH OF DRIED MARJORAM

GRATED ZEST OF ½ ORGANIC LEMON

½ TEASPOON GRATED ORGANIC ORANGE ZEST

9 OUNCES GROUND VEAL

9 OUNCES GROUND PORK

1 TABLESPOON FRESHLY CHOPPED PARSLEY LEAVES

OIL, FOR FRYING

Remove bread crusts. Dice bread and soak in milk in a bowl. Heat oil in skillet and braise diced onion over low heat until transparent. Whisk eggs with mustard, salt and pepper, nutmeg, marjoram, lemon and orange zests.

Mix both kinds of ground meat with soaked bread and the whisked egg mixture. Wet hands, then form palm-sized burgers from the mixture. Heat oil in a skillet and fry both sides of the meat patties over medium heat until fully cooked and golden brown. Remove and drain on a paper towel. Serve as an entrée or in a bun.

SIDE DISHES

Spätzle

Tiny dumplings. Serves 2.

Long dumplings? Fat pasta? Odd-shaped noodles? *Spätzle*, described all of these ways, is a basic starch for soaking up rich gravies and sauces. Some versions are briefly fried after boiling, but not this recipe from chef-owner Philipp Spengel of Heidelberg's Zum Roten Ochsen, a sixth-generation, family-owned restaurant.

1½ CUPS FLOUR

½ TEASPOON SALT

½ TEASPOON NUTMEG

2 EGGS

¼ CUP WATER

1 TEASPOON OIL

[Spätzle, *continued*]

Combine dry ingredients. Add eggs, water, and oil and beat by hand. The dough is ready when bubbles form and all clumps are gone. Consistency should be soft but not too sticky. Boil a pot of water. Push the dough through the larger holes of a sieve or flat grater while carefully holding the sieve or grater above the water. The small dumplings are done in 3–4 minutes, when they float to the top. Drain, then serve.

Kartoffelknödel

Potato dumplings. Serves 6–8.

Chef-owner Philipp Spengel of Zum Roten Ochsen, Heidelberg, also provides this recipe.

2 POUNDS COOKED POTATOES (ABOUT 8)

1 EGG

½ CUP FLOUR

⅛ TEASPOON NUTMEG

1 TEASPOON SALT

MELTED BUTTER

BREAD CRUMBS

Press the potatoes through a ricer and combine with egg. Blend flour with nutmeg and salt. Add mixture to potatoes a little at a time; combine until the dough doesn't stick. Form dumplings into smooth, ¼-cup balls and drop into boiling water, four or five at a time. They are done in 10–15 minutes, when they rise to the top. Note: Don't allow the water to continue to boil after adding the dumplings, or they will fall apart. Remove dumplings with a slotted spoon; top with melted butter and bread crumbs.

Apfelrotkohl

Apples and red cabbage. Serves 4.

What could be more classically German than this mix of sweet and sour indigenous ingredients to round out a hearty meat-and-potatoes meal? Philipp and Anne Spengel, co-owners of Zum Roten Ochsen (Red Ox Inn), Heidelberg, offer this recipe.

1 SMALL RED CABBAGE

1 APPLE

1 CUP RED WINE

1 CUP VINEGAR

1 TEASPOON SALT

1 TEASPOON SUGAR

BOUQUET GARNI OF CLOVES, BAY LEAVES, AND JUNIPER BERRIES

GOOSE FAT*

1 SMALL ONION, SLICED THIN

CORNSTARCH, AS NEEDED

Cut cabbage into wedges. Remove and discard the core, and cut remaining cabbage into thin slices. Peel, core, and slice apple. Marinate cabbage and apple for 1 hour in red wine, vinegar, salt, sugar, and the bouquet garni.

Heat goose fat and glaze the onion slices. Discard bouquet garni. Drain but reserve marinade. Add red cabbage, apple, and ½ cup marinade to onion and cook slowly over medium heat, covered, until soft. Add more marinade as needed to keep moist. Season to taste and thicken (if necessary) with cornstarch.

*A tablespoon of oil or lard may be substituted.

Gemüse-Müsli

Vegetable muesli. Serves 4.

Osnabrück, in Lower Saxony, is situated in a valley between the Wiehen Hills and Teutoburg Forest. It is home to Restaurant la vie, a Relais & Chateaux property where Chef Thomas Bühner uses local ingredients to create a cosmopolitan menu that gains Michelin stars and raves for its artistic appearance. Here is his colorful and novel suggestion for enjoying the root vegetable harvest.

Muesli

½ POUND SMALL POTATOES

½ POUND PARSLEY ROOT

1 FENNEL BULB, ABOUT ⅔ CUP

½ POUND CARROTS

¼ POUND CELERIAC

3 TABLESPOONS TORN FLAT-LEAF PARSLEY (LEAVES ONLY)

2 TEASPOONS COARSELY CHOPPED PECANS

Flavored milk

1 POUND PARSLEY ROOT

3¾–4 CUPS WHOLE MILK

SALT, TO TASTE

[Gemüse-Müsli, *continued*]

Wash and peel the potatoes, parsley root, fennel bulb, carrots, and celeriac. Slice the vegetables thinly, using a grater, and keep separate. Spread the fennel and celeriac out on lightly oiled baking parchment and dry in an oven at 175°F for 60 minutes. The oven door should be left slightly open. Fry other vegetables and the parsley in batches in a deep fat fryer and drain on kitchen paper. Lightly salt all the vegetables.

For the flavored milk, wash and peel the parsley root, then slice into strips using a grater. Add to milk and bring to a boil. Allow the parsley root milk to cool about 10 minutes, and then pass through a sieve. Season to taste. Refrigerate.

Pour the ice-cold milk into cereal bowls, serve, and then add the mixed vegetable flakes and pecans.

Quarkkäulchen mit Apfelmus Crème

Fresh cheese potato pancakes with applesauce cream. Makes 6.

The generous chefs at Leipzig's historic Auerbachs Keller, whose wine bar dates back to 1538, provide this classic German recipe.

Applesauce cream

1 EGG YOLK

1½ TEASPOONS SUGAR

⅓ CUP APPLESAUCE

1 TABLESPOON SOUR CREAM

1 SHEET GELATIN GOLD*

3 TABLESPOONS CALVADOS†

¼ CUP WHIPPING CREAM

Pancakes

½ POUND POTATOES (2 MEDIUM), BOILED IN SKINS, PEELED, AND GRATED

4 OUNCES *QUARK*††

½ CUP FLOUR

2 TEASPOONS SUGAR

1 LARGE EGG

¼ CUP RAISINS

1½ TEASPOONS LEMON JUICE

LEMON ZEST, AS NEEDED

BUTTER

To make the applesauce cream, beat the egg yolk and sugar over heat until it reaches 185°F. Remove from heat and stir until it cools.

Stir the applesauce with the sour cream. Boil the gelatin with the Calvados. Whip the cream. Slowly mix the slightly cooled gelatin-Calvados into the whipped cream. Fold the egg yolk mixture into the applesauce and sour cream. Fold the whipped cream–gelatin mixture into the applesauce mixture. Refrigerate until ready to top the hot pancakes.

To make the pancakes, mix everything (except butter) together well. Melt butter in frying pan. For each pancake, scoop ½ cup of the thick batter into the frying pan and flatten a bit. Fry over medium heat about 2 minutes on each side, or until golden brown and heated through. Serve hot pancakes topped with applesauce cream.

*1 tablespoon unflavored granulated gelatin may be substituted.

†Calvados is an apple brandy from Normandy.

††Ricotta or cream cheese with a little sour cream or yogurt is an adequate substitute.

SAUCES

Currywurst Sauce

Sausage enhancement. Serves many.

This recipe comes from the Deutsches Currywurst Museum, which opened in 2009 to document and celebrate one of Berlin's most beloved street foods. Currywurst booths and food carts are easy to find in the city. Vendors typically slice a hot dog or pork sausage into bite-sized chunks, then douse them with a sauce that resembles a spicy ketchup.

The type of sausage and spiciness of the sauce will depend upon the region of Germany where the *Currywurst* is sold, but no one embraces this quick meal more than Berliners.

¾ CUP WATER

1 HEAPED TEASPOON SUGAR

1½ HEAPED TEASPOONS CURRY POWDER

½ TEASPOON PAPRIKA

1 PINCH SALT

1 TEASPOON RED CHILI PASTE

½ CUP TOMATO PASTE

1 CUP KETCHUP

½ TEASPOON APPLE CIDER VINEGAR

Heat water in pan. Add sugar, curry powder, paprika, salt, chili paste, and tomato paste. Bring to a boil, stirring frequently. Remove pan from heat, stir in ketchup and vinegar, then bring to a boil once more.

[Currywurst Sauce, *continued*]

To serve, cook the sausage of your choice, then cut into bite-sized pieces. Arrange on a plate, top with sauce, and sprinkle with additional curry powder, to taste.

Grüne Soße

Green sauce. Serves 4.

Owner Juan-Enrique Weinhold of The Cooking Ape provides cutting-edge catering in Frankfurt but also embraces local foods and regional heritage. Such is the case with this thick, herbal sauce that Frankfurters love to serve with boiled potatoes and boiled eggs. "Never put onions or garlic in it," the chef advises.

The German writer Goethe (1749–1832) loved *grüne Soße* with boiled potatoes, mentioned it in his books, and helped the sauce become known around the world.

> 2 CUPS FRESH HERBS (A MIX OF CHERVIL, PIMPERNEL, SORREL, BORAGE,
> PARSLEY, CHIVES, AND WATERCRESS)*
>
> 4 TEASPOONS OIL
>
> 3 TEASPOONS VINEGAR OR LIME JUICE
>
> 1 TEASPOON MUSTARD (NOT TOO HOT)
>
> 1 CUP SOUR CREAM
>
> SALT AND PEPPER, TO TASTE
>
> 5 HARD-BOILED EGGS

Chop the fresh herbs. Mix with remaining ingredients, except eggs. Slice eggs in half and remove yolks. Mash yolks and add to herb mixture. Dice egg whites and add to mixture. Chill at least 2 hours.

Tip: Stretch the recipe by using more sour cream or yogurt, but the sauce should be neither runny nor stiff.

*Pimpernel also is known as salad burnet. Some cooks diversify by adding dill, tarragon, lovage, lemon balm, and/or spinach.

DESSERTS

Apfelweinkuchen aus Hessen

Applewine cake from Hesse. Serves many.

Executive chef Andreas Fritsche of the historic Radisson Blu Schwarzer Bock Hotel, Wiesbaden, provides this creamy final course, which uses the alcoholic cider that is Hesse's state beverage and a particular point of pride in Frankfurt's Sachsenhausen area.

Cake dough

2½ CUPS SIFTED FLOUR

½ CUP SUGAR

PINCH SALT

1½ TEASPOONS BAKING POWDER

1 PACKAGE VANILLA SUGAR*

½ CUP BUTTER, SOFTENED

2 EGGS

Filling

5 CUPS SOUR APPLES, PEELED AND DICED†

1½ CUPS COOKIE CRUMBS††

2½ CUPS APPLE WINE

1 CUP CREAM

1½ CUPS SUGAR

1 TABLESPOON CORNSTARCH, FOR THICKENING

For dough, combine dry ingredients, then cream in softened butter. Add eggs and use hands to form semifirm dough. Wrap in plastic wrap and refrigerate for 30 minutes. Preheat oven to 325°F. Grease a 9" springform pan. Roll out dough and line the pan with it, including edges.

For filling, put the apples in a pot, sweat lightly, and add cookie crumbs. Stir. Pour in apple wine and cream; bring to a slow boil. Add sugar, and thicken mixture with cornstarch. The result will be a firm mass.

Distribute apple mixture in springform pan, and bake about 60 minutes. Let cake cool in pan, then use a knife to separate crust from pan. Release sides of springform, carefully loosen cake base with the knife, and slide onto serving platter.

*This is a fine, vanilla-flavored sugar. See page 69 for a recipe to make your own.

†Granny Smith apples work fine.

††Use Butterkeks or Petit Ecolier without chocolate.

Schwarzwälder Kirschtorte

Black Forest cherry torte. Serves 12–14.

One of Germany's most coveted desserts was created by pastry cook Josef Keller near Bonn in 1915. A key ingredient is *Kirschwasser* (cherry schnapps or kirsch), a specialty of the Black Forest.

Chef Benjamin Kunert shares his Hotel Traube Tonbach version of the recipe, which douses cake layers with *Kirschwasser*. Other versions of this classic dessert call for cherries to be soaked in the liquor.

[Schwarzwälder Kirschtorte, *continued*]

Kunert's culinary staff at the five-star Baiersbronn hotel also teach guests how to make *Schwarzwälder Kirschtorte*. This 90-minute cooking class culminates with a taste of the cake, which is not as sweet as it looks, and students take home this recipe. The chef offers additional advice: Completely dissolve the gelatin. Make sure gelatin is not too hot before adding cream. The biscuit cake should not be too dry. Drain syrup from cherries before heating; the cherries will produce additional juice.

Cherry sauce

2 CUPS SOUR CHERRIES (SUCH AS A JAR OF SCHATTENMORELLEN)

1¼ CUPS CHERRY SYRUP (FROM ABOVE), DIVIDED

¼ CUP SUGAR

¼ CUP WHEAT STARCH OR CORNSTARCH

Chocolate biscuit crust

6 EGGS

½ CUP SUGAR

½ CUP FLOUR

½ CUP WHEAT STARCH OR CORNSTARCH

¼ CUP COCOA POWDER

½ TEASPOON BAKING POWDER

Chocolate-sable cake

3 EGG YOLKS

½ CUP SUGAR

½ CUP SOFT BUTTER

2 PINCHES OF SALT

1¼ CUPS FLOUR

¼ CUP COCOA POWDER

3 TEASPOONS BAKING POWDER

Kirsch foam

5 SHEETS OF GELATIN*

⅓ CUP *KIRSCHWASSER*

⅓ CUP SUGAR

3 CUPS WHIPPED CREAM

Topping

KIRSCHWASSER, TO TASTE

1¾ CUPS WHIPPED CREAM

SHAVED CHOCOLATE

CANDIED CHERRIES

To make the cherry sauce, drain cherries, but reserve the syrup. Mix ½ cup syrup with sugar and wheat starch or cornstarch; set aside. Briefly heat remaining syrup in saucepan, then add the syrup mixture. Constantly stir until sauce thickens; this will not take long over medium heat. Add drained cherries. Set aside.
For the chocolate biscuit crust, preheat oven to 350°F. Cover bottom of a springform pan with parchment paper. Heat eggs and sugar in the top of a double boiler that has 100°F water, whisking until creamy. Sift remaining crust ingredients and gently fold into the egg mixture. Pour mixture into the springform pan and bake for 35 minutes. When cool, slice the biscuit into three thin layers layers.
For chocolate-sable dough, whip yolks and sugar with an electric mixer. Add butter and salt. Sift flour, cocoa powder, and baking powder. Fold dry ingredients into the egg mixture. Refrigerate for 1 hour, then roll out dough into a circle, ⅛" thick and the same size as the biscuit crust. It is easier to roll out the dough on a greased cookie sheet.
Preheat oven to 350°F and bake the sable base about 12 minutes. Loosen cake from sheet and let cool.
For the kirsh foam, melt the gelatin and *Kirschwasser* with the sugar on a stovetop. Cool slightly. Take ¾ cup of the whipped cream and add to the mixture (which should be no hotter than 95°F). Fold in the remaining whipped cream.
To assemble, use the chocolate sable cake as the base. Drench with *Kirschwasser*. Spread the cherry sauce on top. Cover the cherries with one-third of the kirsh foam. Top with the bottom chocolate biscuit slice, drench with kirsh and spread one-half of the remaining kirsh foam. Repeat. Refrigerate about 2 hours. Add remaining chocolate biscuit slice and cover with 1–1½ cups whipped cream. Garnish with shaved chocolate, candied cherries, and rosettes of whipped cream.
*Two envelopes unflavored gelatin powder may be substituted.

Zimtsterne

Christmas cinnamon stars. Makes 2 dozen.
The origin of this popular and rich cookie can be traced back to the Swabian region of Bavaria, but it shows up nearly everywhere in Germany during the Advent season. This recipe comes from the German National Tourism Office.

2¼ CUPS WHOLE ALMONDS*

5 EGG WHITES

2 CUPS CONFECTIONER'S SUGAR, SIFTED

2 TEASPOONS GROUND CINNAMON

1 TABLESPOON KIRSCH (CHERRY SCHNAPPS)

ADDITIONAL CONFECTIONER'S SUGAR

[Zimtsterne, *continued*]

Scald almonds with boiling water, remove their skins, and allow to cool. Grind fine. Beat egg whites until stiff peaks form. Gently fold in confectioner's sugar and set aside 1–1½ cups of the mixture. To the remaining egg mixture, fold in ground almonds, cinnamon, and kirsch, then quickly form a dough. Let dough rest, covered, for one hour in the refrigerator.

Cover a work surface with sugar and roll out chilled dough to ½" thick. Use a 2½" star-pattern cookie cutter to form cookies. Cover each star evenly and thickly with reserved egg-sugar mixture, place on an ungreased cookie sheet, and let all uncooked cookies dry overnight at room temperature.

Preheat oven to 425°F and bake cookies for 5 minutes, at most. Check often; the cookie tops should stay white and the insides should remain soft.

*Slivered almonds cut prep time because no scalding or skin removal is needed.

Vanillekipferl

Vanilla crescents. Makes about 3 dozen.

These melt-in-your-mouth treats, which have an Austrian origin, are a German holiday favorite. This recipe comes from the German National Tourism Office.

3½ TABLESPOONS UNPEELED ALMONDS

3½ TABLESPOONS HAZELNUTS

1¼ CUPS FLOUR

¼ CUP PLUS 1 TABLESPOON SUGAR

PINCH SALT

½ CUP PLUS 6 TABLESPOONS BUTTER, COLD AND CUT INTO SMALL PIECES

2 EGG YOLKS

5 PACKETS VANILLA SUGAR*

½ CUP POWDERED SUGAR

Pour boiling water over the almonds; remove the skins and chop fine. Finely chop the hazelnuts. Sift the flour onto a large wooden board. Make a well in the flour and add the almonds, hazelnuts, sugar, and salt. Blend, then add butter and egg yolks. Knead the dough until it is smooth and pliable, but do not over-knead. Wrap the dough in aluminum foil and let rest for 2 hours in the refrigerator.

Preheat the oven to 375°F. Divide the dough and form into several pencil-thick rolls. Cut the rolls into 2" lengths and bend into crescent shapes. Place on cookie sheets and bake on a middle rack until golden brown, about 10 minutes.

Stir vanilla sugar and powdered sugar together in a shallow bowl. Carefully dip still-warm crescent cookies in the sugar mixture.

Suggestion: To store the cookies so they won't break, use waxed paper to separate layers stacked in a cookie tin.

*One packet of vanilla sugar equals 1 tablespoon. To make your own, slice a vanilla bean, open it and remove the seeds. Mix the seeds with 2 cups of sugar in an airtight container for 1–2 weeks before using.

Ofenschlüpfer

Sweet bread pudding. Serves 6–12.

Amidst the twisting lanes and streets of Old Town Baden-Baden is a charming wine bar and restaurant that is a favorite of local residents. The Weinstube im Baldreit exudes an earthy, friendly vibe and is among the area's less-expensive dining options. Relax in the courtyard when weather cooperates, or head to the cozy, softly lit cellar for *Flammkuchen* (pizza) to *Bachsaibling* (brook trout) with lemon-caper butter. Adventurous? The restaurant's specialties include *Saumagen* (pig's stomach) stuffed with ground pork, potatoes, and carrots (the stomach is discarded after the entrée is baked).

As a final course, chef Philipp Fouillé offers this twist on a classic recipe.

Bread pudding

1 CUP MILK

¼ CUP SUGAR

2 CUPS LIGHTLY TOASTED AND CUBED STALE BREAD ROLLS

2 EGGS

1 PEELED APPLE, SLICED FINE

⅓ CUP RAISINS

¼ CUP ROASTED ALMOND SLICES

1 TEASPOON BAKING POWDER

Caramel cream

¾ CUP SUGAR

1½ TABLESPOONS WATER

1¼ CUPS CREAM

7 OUNCES CURD CHEESE*

½ VANILLA BEAN

7 OUNCES CURD CHEESE*

QUART OF VANILLA ICE CREAM

Preheat oven to 300°F. Butter 12 muffin cups.

For pudding, mix milk and sugar. Heat and bring to a boil. Pour over bread cubes and let stand 15 minutes. Combine eggs, apple slices, raisins, almonds, and baking powder. Fold the fruit mix into the bread mix. Fill muffin tins.

[Ofenschlüpfer, *continued*]

Fill a baking pan with 2" of water and place it on the bottom oven rack. Set the muffin pan on the middle oven rack and bake for 40 minutes.
To make caramel cream, heat sugar and water in saucepan until mixture caramelizes, then add cream to deglaze pan ingredients. Add vanilla bean and refrigerate mixture. When it is cold, whip the caramel cream and fold in curd cheese (or cream cheese).
Use an icing bag to arrange the caramel-cream on serving plates. Add a warm bread pudding or two, plus a scoop of ice cream.
*Curd cheese is similar to cream cheese, but the fat content is lower. Cream cheese is an adequate substitute.

Nürnberger Elisenlebkuchen

Nuremberg gingerbread (without flour). Makes about 100 cookies.

The world's oldest written recipe for gingerbread, from the 16th century, can be found at the Germanic National Museum. This is a translation from Nuremberg, the Bavarian city where gingerbread was created, and the recipe is provided through the German National Tourist Office.

Note that the ingredients do not include flour. After the cookies are baked, they must rest at least a week before they are ready to eat. Store them covered with a piece of parchment paper in a cookie tin. Place a small apple slice or apple peel on top of the paper, or place an orange in the tin.

Use parchment paper and *Oblaten,* thin and edible disks that resemble communion wafers, to lessen dough spreading and ease the removal of the cookies from baking sheets.

1 CUP SUGAR

6 LARGE EGGS

1 TEASPOON VANILLA

½ CUP HONEY

½ TEASPOON CINNAMON

½ TEASPOON GROUND CLOVES

½ TEASPOON GROUND CORIANDER

½ TEASPOON ALLSPICE

½ TEASPOON MACE

½ TEASPOON CARDAMOM

2½ CUPS COARSELY GROUND ALMONDS

2½ CUPS FINELY GROUND HAZELNUTS

½ CUPS CHOPPED WALNUTS

1 CUP FINELY CHOPPED CANDIED ORANGE PEEL

1 CUP FINELY CHOPPED CANDIED LEMON PEEL

1 TABLESPOON FINELY CHOPPED CANDIED GINGER, OPTIONAL

2¾-INCH (70 MM) *OBLATEN* DISKS

Optional glaze

8 OUNCES DARK CHOCOLATE, OR

1¼ CUPS POWDERED SUGAR MIXED WITH 3 TABLESPOONS WATER

Optional toppings

WHOLE ALMONDS, PEELED

CANDIED CHERRIES

Place the sugar, eggs, and vanilla in a bowl and beat until the sugar dissolves. Stir the honey gently into the mixture. Then add the spices, nuts, and candied orange, lemon, and (if desired) ginger peel.

Place a heaping teaspoon of dough on each *Oblate,* then spread to leave only a slight rim uncovered. Let sit for about 40 minutes in a dry, warm room.

Preheat the oven to 375°F. Place dough-topped *Oblaten* on a parchment-covered baking sheet. Bake 12 to 15 minutes, until golden brown, but dough should not be baked completely through.

Cool on a rack. After gingerbread cools, it can be glazed and decorated. Dip into melted chocolate, or make a sugar glaze by mixing sugar and water, then heating to 225°F. The cookies also can be stored and eaten without a glaze.

Nürnberger Lebkuchen

Nuremberg gingerbread or honey cookies (with flour). Makes 6 dozen 2½-inch cookies. This version of gingerbread, also provided by the German National Tourist Office, uses some of the same spices as the flourless recipe, but the result is a dough that is rolled instead of spooned onto cookie sheets.

¼ CUP HONEY

2 TABLESPOONS BUTTER, SOFTENED

4 EGGS

4¾ CUPS SUGAR, DIVIDED

3⅓ CUPS FLOUR

1 TABLESPOON BAKING POWDER

1 TEASPOON GROUND CARDAMOM

1 TEASPOON GROUND CLOVES

1 TEASPOON GROUND CINNAMON

[Nürnberger Lebkuchen, *continued*]

FLOUR, AS NEEDED

MILK

OPTIONAL: POWDERED SUGAR GLAZE, CANDIED CHERRIES, WHOLE AND
PEELED ALMONDS, SPRINKLES

In a medium-sized pan, warm honey and butter slowly until the butter melts completely.
Beat the eggs until frothy. Slowly add 3½ cups sugar to the eggs.
Mix the flour, baking powder, and spices. Add the honey–butter mix and egg–sugar
cream to the flour. Knead the mixture and refrigerate for an hour.
Preheat oven to 350°F. On a floured surface, roll out the dough to a thickness of ¼"
and cut it into hearts or gingerbread men.
Place the cookies on a parchment-covered baking sheet and brush them with a
small amount of milk. Bake 10–15 minutes (depending on cookie size).
After cookies have cooled, coat them with a powdered sugar glaze and/or other
decorations as desired.

Apfelkücherl

Apple fritters. Makes 12–18.

Chef Alfons Schuhbeck of Munich notes that this hot and simple treat can be
prepared with a wine- or beer-batter coating instead of this choux pastry recipe. He
notes that when Bavarians use elderflowers instead of apple rings, the fritters are
called *Hollerkücherl*.

¾ CUP MILK, DIVIDED

¼ CUP WATER

3 TABLESPOONS BUTTER

PINCH OF SALT

1 CUP SIFTED FLOUR

3 EGGS

⅓ CUP SUGAR

1½ TEASPOONS GROUND CINNAMON

3 SOUR APPLES

1⅔ CUPS FAT FOR FRYING

Boil ¼ cup of the milk, water, butter, and salt in a small saucepan. Pour flour into
saucepan, stirring constantly for about 1 minute or until batter separates from
bottom of saucepan. Transfer batter to a bowl and gradually stir in eggs and
remaining milk until batter is smooth and thick.

Mix sugar and cinnamon. Peel and core apples, then cut apples crossways into ½-inch rings. Heat fat to 350°F in a deep skillet or deep-fat fryer. (When it is hot enough, small bubbles form around the handle of a wooden spoon.) Dip apple slices into batter, let excess drip off, and fry until golden brown. Remove the *Apfelkücherl* with a skimmer, drain briefly on paper towels and immediately turn over in cinnamon sugar.

Niederegger Gentlemen's Dream

Serves 4.

Niederegger Lübeck produces 30 tons of marzipan (a mix of ground almonds, sugar, and a mystery ingredient) each day, and the work has happened in the same spot for more than 200 years. The seventh-generation family business also maintains a Marzipan Museum with amazing sculptures made from the confection. A marzipan artist works with the sweet dough as visitors watch and ask questions. Downstairs is a café where luscious, many-layered cakes are the stars.

The treats are exported to 35 countries, and many of the 300 products require chocolate, which brings us to this Niederegger Lübeck recipe—one of many that are shared. The marzipan recipe, though, remains top secret. Only four people know the secret ingredient.

2 CUPS VANILLA PUDDING

3 SACHETS NIEDEREGGER DRINKING CHOCOLATE, DIVIDED*

3½ OUNCES DARK CHOCOLATE

3 TABLESPOONS RUM

¾ CUP WHIPPING CREAM

Prepare vanilla pudding from your favorite recipe or pudding mix. Reserve four teaspoons of drinking chocolate powder and stir the remainder into the warm pudding. Cover pudding with plastic wrap and leave to cool.

Chop the dark chocolate. Stir chocolate and rum into pudding. Whip cream until stiff and slowly fold half of it into pudding. Place alternate layers of the pudding-cream and remaining whipped cream in four dessert glasses. Chill 1 hour in the refrigerator. To serve, top with remaining chocolate powder and chocolate shavings, if desired.
*Equals about ½ cup of sweetened cocoa mix.

Pflaumenkuchen

Plum cake. Serves 6–8.

Michelle Clasen-Werry completed pastry chef training at Fassbender Bakery in Siegburg, Germany. Today she operates Clasen's European Bakery, which her father Ralf Clasen and uncle Ernst Clasen established in Middleton, Wisconsin, in 1959 after emigrating from Cologne, Germany. The bakery specializes in authentic Old World pastries, breads, tortes, and candies.

[Pflaumenkuchen, *continued*]

Germany's plum season, late summer to early autumn, results in plenty of plum cake throughout the country. It also is sold at Clasen's, and this simplified version of the bakery recipe is easy to make at home.

Dough

1½ CUPS FLOUR

½ CAKE FRESH YEAST

2 TABLESPOONS SUGAR

PINCH OF SALT

⅓ CUP MILK

2 TABLESPOONS BUTTER

FLOUR, FOR KNEADING

MARGARINE OR BUTTER

Topping

1 POUND ITALIAN PRUNE PLUMS*

1 TABLESPOON SUGAR

½ TEASPOON CINNAMON

Sift the flour into a bowl, and make a well in the center. Crumble in the yeast, and then sprinkle in the sugar and salt. Pour milk into a small saucepan, add butter, and heat gently until butter melts. Pour over yeast. Use your hands to knead the ingredients until you have smooth dough. Cover with a clean cloth and leave in a warm place for 30 to 40 minutes until dough doubles in volume.

Preheat oven to 350ºF. Use margarine or butter to grease an 8½" springform pan. Knead dough well on a floured surface, and roll out until it is only slightly larger than the pan's bottom. Place dough in pan, drawing the sides up only slightly. Wash plums, then halve them and remove the pits. Arrange on the dough, cut side facing up. Bake 1 hour.

Combine cinnamon and sugar; sprinkle over the hot cake. Cool in the pan.

*Although the smaller Italian prune plums are preferred, other types of plums can be substituted.

Shopping in Germany's Food Markets

Helpful Tips

Outdoor Markets

Farmers' markets show up everywhere in Germany, from rural villages to metropolitan neighborhoods, and a market stroll is an excellent way to see and sample regional specialties. Expect to see beautiful displays of fresh vegetables, fruits, cheeses, and sausage garlands at these plentiful, outdoor emporiums. Do not expect to haggle about price; Germans are not known for their love of bartering.

Each season brings its unique flavors, which include fat stalks of white asparagus in spring, currants and gooseberries in summer, apples and pears in autumn.

All year, the weekly Hamburg *Fischmarkt* at the city's harbor, next to an historic fish auction house, provides excellent food theater in addition to sustenance. Many fishermen hawk their catches—eel, herring, and much more—in an animated manner during these fun and popular Sunday morning gatherings, which have commenced for more than 300 years. Inside the auction house is a mix of live music from local musicians, beer, and sausage sandwiches. Fish sales occur in booths outdoors.

Viktualienmarkt, open since 1807, is the oldest open-air market in Munich. Look for nearly 150 booths in the Old Town area during daytime business hours. Yes, there also is a beer garden, but both it and the market are closed on Sundays.

Some farmers' markets, including the *Viktualienmarkt,* are open all year. Others are seasonal, and their openings mark the arrival of spring. All benefit from the activities of Slow Food Germany, which presents the annual *Markt des guten Geschmacks* (Market for Good Taste) every April in Stuttgart. More than 400 artisan food producers participate and at least 50,000 foodies and potential customers attend workshops, field trips, and specialty meals.

Slow Food Germany's other major food extravaganza is *SlowFisch* (SlowFish), which promotes sustainable fishing and fish markets. The event occurs in Bremen in November.

During the Advent season, hundreds of *Christkindlmarkts*—outdoor Christmas markets—emerge to acknowledge the impending holiday. The *Weihnachtsmarkt* in Frankfurt, among the nation's oldest and biggest *Christkindlmarkts,* has been around since 1393.

Bite into steaming, foot-long sausages and sip mugs of *Glühwein* (warmed, mulled wine) or *Äppelwoi* (hot cider) with the locals during these festive yuletide events. Take home large, heart-shaped cookies of gingerbread, inscribed with a holiday greeting and affixed to ribbon, so they can be worn like a necklace.

The gatherings are as much about taking time to visit with neighbors as they are seasonal shopping extravaganzas where handicrafts, especially religious items, are sold. The holiday markets also are a good place to purchase traditional holiday candies and cookies. Local musicians typically play Christmas music in the background or in concert at a nearby church.

Specialty festivals before Christmas are devoted to food. An example is the annual Stollen Festival in early December in Dresden. The highlight is a parade through Old Town; hundreds of local pastry chefs walk with an enormous Christmas cake. The 2012 version was the world's biggest at 4 tons and 13 feet in length. The giant cake is made up of hundreds of handmade *Stollen* that are joined together as one piece of art. After the parade, a 26-pound, 5-foot-long and silver-plated *Stollenmesser* (stollen knife) is used to ceremoniously cut into the cake. Slices of yeasty fruitcake are sold to thousands of spectators.

Less publicized, globally, are Germany's *Ostermarkts* during the weeks preceding Easter. Elaborately decorated wooden, plastic or real (hollowed out) eggs are sold, as are holiday cookies, chocolate candy, and lamb-shaped cakes. Water fountains in city centers are decorated with wreaths, garland strands, and colored eggs.

Eggs are seen as a symbol of new life, and the rabbit represents fertility in Germany. It is not unusual for German families to decorate an *Osterbaum* (Easter tree), indoors or outdoors, with colorful eggs and garland. The *Osterhase* (Easter bunny) leaves children little treats on Easter Sunday.

Indoor Markets

One-stop shopping is not as commonplace in Germany as it is in the United States. The butcher, baker, and other food specialists remain valued for the expertise and quality of the products produced.

At the opposite extreme are mega food stores that are widely known for their range of specialties and excellent quality. The best provide room for leisurely eating onsite, in addition to foods to prepare at home.

Consider the KaDeWe (*Kaufhaus des Westens*) department store in Berlin, which is a splendid tourist attraction as well as an exquisite place to shop. KaDeWe presents a sensational array of gourmet specialty foods, including indigenous German products, on its sixth floor. Open since 1907 and as big as nine football fields, the store also makes room for chef stations and dining in several nooks adjacent to where ingredients are sold.

In Munich, the family-owned *Dallmayr* earns a reputation for being one of the world's best-known and extensive delicatessens, but many specialty foods and beverages also are sold there. The business is enormous but has no central cashier. Customers purchase products in each department where they are stocked.

Any city of major size will have a hub for gourmet and exotic food specialties, but size certainly is not the only hallmark of excellence. Consider *Faber Feinkost*, Bad Kissingen, which has produced sausages since 1898 and ranks among Germany's most highly regarded gourmet food and butcher shops. Bad Kissingen, with a population that hovers around 20,000, is in Bavaria's Lower Franconia and at the near-center of Germany.

Average grocery stores for average people also exist, of course, and—as in most countries—authentic and inexpensive souvenirs are just a matter of browsing the aisles.

If you are tempted to bring unpackaged food back to the United States, obtain the Customs and Border Protection (CPB) brochure "Know Before You Go," to find out which agricultural items are allowed. Ask for this brochure at 877-CBP-5511 or find the information online at www.cbp.gov (search for "know before you go").

About Street Eats

The motto "Cleanliness is next to Germanness" has long been quoted in books, embroidered on dish towels, and considered a core priority for German households and businesses. The deeply engrained stereotype remains a part of Germany's national identity, and this extends to food prepared for commercial sales.

Germany is a nation that takes great pride in its outdoor community markets and festivals. Public sanitation standards are high. It is highly unlikely that food vendors will sell products that are unsafe for visitors to eat. They are more likely to be meticulous about product consistency and quality, but—as anywhere in the world—always be aware of cooking conditions and use common sense before purchasing a street snack. Bottled water is readily available, and Germany's per-capita consumption is the fifth highest in the world. Tap water, although held to a high standard of quality by the government, is not typically served at restaurants.

Weights and Measures

Germans use the metric system and pay with euros. Dry products are priced by the gram or kilogram. Beverages and other liquids are measured in liters. Use this abbreviated list of approximate weights to obtain the desired quantities:

Gramm: 1 gram, or 0.035 ounces (1 ounce requires about 28 grams.)

Dekagramm: 10 grams

Kilogramm: 1,000 grams, or 2.2 pounds

Schoppen: 0.5 liters, or about 17 ounces (usually a beer measurement)

Liter: 1 liter, or about 34 ounces

Scheffel: roughly 50 liters, comparable to 1.4 U.S. bushels

Hektoliter: 1 hectoliter, or 100 liters.

Old-time German measurements include the *Pfund* (pound), which is 500 *Gramm* and slightly heavier than the U.S. pound (454 grams). The traditional German *Quart* (quart) is 38.7 ounces, or 1.14 liters. It is slightly more than the U.S. quart, which is 32 fluid ounces, or 0.95 liters.

Resources

Suppliers of German Food Items

Most of the special ingredients required for the recipes in this book (see *Tastes of Germany,* p. 43) are available from online suppliers of German food products. Several of these businesses are based in the United States and stock an impressive array of fresh, frozen, cured, smoked, and tinned products: sausages and other meats, cheeses, preserves, sauces, krauts, and other condiments. Baking needs and baked goods also are available. Also notable: Wisconsin-based Bavaria Sausage, Inc. ships all-in-one German specialty meals (such as *Sauerbraten, Kassler Ripchen,* and *Rouladen*), to "take the fuss out of cooking."

Among the larger purveyors of German food products are:

Amana Meat Market
800-373-6328
www.amanashops.com
shipping@amanashops.com

Bavaria Sausage, Inc.
800-733-6695
www.bavariasausage.com
sales@bavariasausage.com

German Gourmet
877-437-4687
www.germangourmet.com
info@germangourmet.com

German Grocery
800-262-2253
www.germangrocery.com
sales@germangrocery.com

GermanShop24.com
(no phone orders; based in Germany)
www.germanshop24.com
info@germanshop24.com

Stiglmeier Sausage Co.
800-451-8199
www.stiglmeier.com
sales@stiglmeier.com

The Taste of Germany
800-881-6419
www.thetasteofgermany.com
contact@thetasteofgermany.com

Usinger's Sausage
800-558-9998
www.usinger.com

Suppliers of specialty game meats:

Red Stag Acres
608-857-3386
www.redstagacres.com
info@redstagacres.com
Mike or Mary Gilbert, owners
(Farm-raised reindeer and elk)

Gooch Farms
262-593-5806
goochfarms@hotmail.com
John Gooch, owner
(Farm-raised European red deer)

Specialty Meats & Gourmet
800-310-2360
www.smgfoods.com
(Farm-raised Midwest and New Zealand
deer; various other meats and game birds)

These businesses specialize in German-made equipment for cooking and baking:

Chantal Cookware
800-365-4354
www.chantal.com
orders@chantalcorp.com

Fissler
888-FISSLER
www.fissler.com
info@fisslerusa.com

Tours and Travel Advice

The German National Tourist Board provides well-organized, helpful, and extensive online resources to assist travelers with myriad interests, including culinary tourism.

For ambitious, active vacationers, themed bicycle trails include the Baden and Lower Saxony asparagus routes (where much of the ubiquitous spring crop is grown), the German Cabbage Route (near the North Sea coast), and the Schleswig-Holstein Cheese Route (connecting 30 dairies). Other routes, also accessible via car, snake through major wine regions.

In addition, eat-the-world city tours delve into the regional specialties and cultural history of Germany's major urban areas, including Berlin and Munich. Reservations are necessary for these popular excursions. Private tours also are arranged.

eat-the-world
49 (0) 30 530 661 65
www.eat-the-world.com
info@eat-the-world.com

In Heidelberg, Susanne Fiek arranges customized tours to match the interests of travelers in the area, and choices include a culinary/wine emphasis.

event & event...chen Heidelberg
(Events great and small in Heidelberg)
49 (0) 62 21 86 73 580
www.eventchen-heidelberg.de
fiek@eventchen-heidelberg.de

Useful Organizations and Travel Resources

German Government and Tourism Offices

Embassy of the Federal Republic of Germany
2300 M St. NW
Washington, DC 20037
202-298-4000
www.germany.info
Use web form to submit questions or write to gicinfo@germanembassy.us

Germany National Tourist Office
122 E. 42nd St., Suite 2000
New York, NY 10168
212-661-7200
www.cometogermany.com
germanyinfo@germany.travel

German Consulate General, Midwest U.S.
676 N. Michigan Ave., Suite 3200
Chicago, IL 60611
312-202-0480
chicago@germany-info.org

DANK Haus German American Cultural Center, Chicago, is home to the Midwest German Consulate General and offers more than 150 public cultural programs each year. For more information, consult www.dankhous.com or 773-561-9181.

International Organizations

Two non-profit, international travel organizations, The Friendship Force and Servas, promote goodwill and understanding among people of different cultures. These organizations share similar ideals but operate somewhat differently. Friendship Force members travel in groups to host countries. Both itinerary and travel arrangements are made by a member acting as exchange director. These trips combine stays with a host family and group travel within the host country. Servas members travel independently and make their own contacts with fellow members in other countries, choosing hosts with attributes of interest from membership rosters.

For more information about membership in these groups:

Friendship Force International
127 Peachtree St., Suite 501
Atlanta, GA 30303
404-522-9490
404-688-6148 (fax)
www.thefriendshipforce.org

US Servas, Inc.
1125 16th St., Suite 201
Arcata, CA 95521
707-825-1714
info@usservas.org
www.usservas.org

TOP LEFT *Nürnberger Bratwürste* (roasted links of Nuremberg bratwurst) arrive with *Sauerkraut* and *Kartoffeln gebraten* (golden fried potatoes) at the Joh. Albrecht Brauhaus, Hamburg. **TOP RIGHT** Chef Grit Jossunek presents a sampler of traditional Hessen appetizers at the Restaurant Zur Pfalz, Schriesheim. **MIDDLE** Diners linger inside and out at the Fisch Küche at Laboe, on the Baltic Sea. **BOTTOM LEFT** *Zwiebelkuchen* (onion tart or cake) is a German specialty in autumn; this one comes from Café König, Baden Baden. **BOTTOM RIGHT** The sixth-generation Zum Roten Ochsen, Heidelberg, is popular with college students.

TOP LEFT Berliners love *Currywurst*, sausage chunks doused with a spiced, tomato-based sauce. It is popular street-vendor fare. **TOP RIGHT** A clay gingerbread house signifies the arrival of the *Christkindlmarkt* season in Regensburg. **BOTTOM LEFT** *Senf* (mustard) is a major product in Bautzen, a Sorbian city that also operates a mustard museum. **BOTTOM RIGHT** A frothy latte, poured in Frankfurt, arrives with a nibble of something sweet. Little *Kekse* (cookies) often accompany hot beverages in Germany.

TOP LEFT *Spargel* (asparagus) fills spring markets. **TOP RIGHT** Schiffer Café, Kiel, serves cold *Matjes* (marinated herring). **MIDDLE** *Entenbrust* (duck breast) arrives rare at a Porsche factory meal near Leipzig. **BOTTOM LEFT** Regensburg's Salzstadel is the world's oldest sausage kitchen. **BOTTOM RIGHT** Traube Tonbach, Baiersbronn, serves *schwarzwälder Kirschtorte* (Black Forest cherry torte).

TOP LEFT Executive chef Dirk Schröer of Caroussel, Dresden, adds a contemporary spin to German cuisine. **TOP RIGHT** A German city's *Ratskeller* (or *Rathskeller*), which serves hearty food and beer, typically is below street level and historically was below the city hall. Here is the entrance to Munich's. **BOTTOM** Steaming *Glühwein* (warm and spiced wine) is served outdoors during the *Christkindlmarkt* in Mariakirchen, a Bavarian village about 80 miles northeast of Munich.

TOP LEFT *Reibekuchen mit Nordseekrabben, Sauerrahm, und Salatbeilage* (potato pancakes with shrimp, sour cream, and salad) at Café Elbterrassen, Hamburg. **TOP RIGHT** Baden-Baden's Steigenberger Europäischer Hof serves *Weißwürstchen* (white sausages) for breakfast. **MIDDLE** The third-generation Hotel Bareiss, Baiersbronn, earns Michelin stars. **BOTTOM LEFT** Jörg Sackmann is chef-owner of Hotel Sackmann, a wellness retreat in Baiersbronn. **BOTTOM RIGHT** At LeBuffet, Kiel, the spread includes creamy asparagus soup.

TOP LEFT *Himberren* (raspberries), *Johannisbeeren* (currants, shown), *Stachelbeeren* (gooseberries), *Heidelbeeren* (blueberries), *Sauerkirschen* (sour cherries), and *Erdbeeren* (strawberries, shown) are fresh, plump, and plentiful at an outdoor market in Berlin. **TOP RIGHT** Customers can watch *Honiglebkuchen* (gingerbread) decorated on the spot during a *Christkindlmarkt* in Munich. **BOTTOM** *Dresdner Stollen* is a specialty at Scheinert Bakery, Dresden, and the sweetened Christmas bread is one of Saxony's biggest exports. The European Union categorizes it as a regionally distinctive and protected product.

TOP LEFT *Schweinefilet eingewickelt in Rouladenfleisch* (pork filets wrapped in pounded beef filets) is sold at Berlin's vast KaDeWe department store, where one floor is devoted to food. **TOP RIGHT** Chef Claus-Peter Lumpp has earned Michelin stars at the Hotel Bareiss, Baiersbronn. **MIDDLE LEFT** Deidesheimer Hof, Neustadt, serves braised *Kalbsbäckchen* (veal cheeks) with gnocchi for lunch. **BOTTOM** Life-sized sculptures are carved from marzipan, sweetened almond paste, at the Niederegger company museum in Lübeck.

TOP LEFT Dainty portions of foie gras gain a Coca-Cola glacé and lemon sorbet topping at Caroussel, Dresden. **TOP RIGHT** Sylvia Knösel of Chocolatier Knösel sells the Heidelberger *Studentenkuss* (the Heidelberg Student's Kiss), a candy with a sweet story that dates back to the 1800s. **BOTTOM LEFT** Restaurant Zur Pflaz, Schriesheim, serves a German take on the Spanish "tapas," an assortment of cold sausages, cheese, and pickled vegetables. **BOTTOM RIGHT** This mocha-flavored cake with vanilla mousse filling and marzipan coating is a popular treat at Café Maldaner, Wiesbaden.

Helpful Phrases

For Use in Restaurants and Food Markets

In the Restaurant

Although many Germans speak English, your attempts to speak the native language will be appreciated, especially when a question ends with the word "please" (*bitte*). It is a sign of respect and goodwill. Use these questions when referring to Germany's foods. Phonetic translations help with pronunciation; syllables in capital letters are accented. Note that the ß sounds like an "ss," the ch is pronounced like the Scottish "ch" in "Loch" or like the "h" in "huge," the ü resembles either the "ew" or "uh," the ö equals "er," and the ä is either "ai" or "eh." All nouns are capitalized.

DO YOU HAVE A MENU, PLEASE?

Haben Sie eine Speisekarte, bitte?
HAH-behn zee eye-nuh SHPEYE-zuh-KAHR-tuh, BITT-tuh?

MAY I SEE THE MENU, PLEASE?

Darf ich die Speisekarte anschauen, bitte?
Dahrf ikh dee SHPEYE-zuh-KAHR-tuh AHN-shou-en, BITT-tuh?

WHAT DO YOU RECOMMEND TODAY?

Was empfehlen Sie heute?
Vahs ehmp-FAY-lehn zee HOI-tuh?

DO YOU HAVE . . . ?
(ADD AN ITEM FROM THE *MENU GUIDE* OR THE *FOODS & FLAVORS GUIDE*.)

Haben Sie . . . ?
HAH-behn zee . . . ?

83

HELPFUL PHRASES

RESTAURANT

WHAT IS THE "SPECIAL" FOR
TODAY, PLEASE?

Was ist das Tagesmenü, bitte?
*Vahs ist dahs TAH-ges-meh-NEW,
BITT-tuh?*

DO YOU HAVE ANY SPECIAL
LOCAL DISHES?

Haben Sie Spezialitäten aus der
Gegend?
*HAH-behn zee SHPEH-tsy-AH-lee-
TAY-tehn ows dair GAY-gehnt?*

IS THIS DISH SPICY?

Ist dieses Gericht scharf?
Ist dee-zehs geh-REEKHT shahrf?

MAY I/WE ORDER . . . ?

Darf ich/Dürfen wir . . . bestellen?
*Dahrf ikh/DUHR-fehn vihr . . . beh-
SHTEH-lehn?*

WHAT ARE THE INGREDIENTS IN
THIS DISH, PLEASE?

Was sind die Zutaten in diesem
Gericht, bitte?
*Vahs zint dee zuh-TA-ten in dee-
zem geh-REEKHT, BITT-tuh?*

WHAT ARE THE SEASONINGS IN
THIS DISH, PLEASE?

Was sind die Gewürze in diesem
Gericht, bitte?
*Vahs zint dee geh-VUHRT-tsuh in
dee-zem geh-REEKHT, BITT-tuh?*

THANK YOU VERY MUCH. THE
FOOD IS DELICIOUS.

Danke sehr. Das Essen ist hervorragend.
*DAHN-kuh zair. Dahs EH-sen ist
HAIR-fohr-RAH-gehnt.*

84

In the Market

Consult this list when making purchases or trying to learn more about unfamiliar ingredients.

WHAT ARE THE REGIONAL FRUITS AND VEGETABLES?	Was sind die Obst- und Gemüsearten aus der Gegend? *Vahs zint dee Ohpst uhnt geh-MEW-zeh-AHR-tehn ows dair GAY-gehnt?*
WHAT IS THIS CALLED?	Wie heißt das? *Vee hyst dahs?*
DO YOU SELL . . . HERE? (ADD AN ITEM FROM THE *FOODS & FLAVORS GUIDE*.)	Verkaufen Sie . . . hier? *Fair-KOW-fehn zee . . . heer?*
MAY I TASTE THIS?	Darf ich das bitte probieren? *Dahrf ikh dahs BITT-tuh pro-BEE-rehn?*
WHERE CAN I BUY FRESH . . . ?	Wo kann ich frische . . . kaufen? *Voh kahn ikh frih-shuh . . . KOW-fehn?*
HOW MUCH IS THIS PER KILOGRAM?	Wieviel kostet das per Kilo? *Vee-feel KAWS-teht dahs pair KEE-loh?*
TWO HUNDRED FIFTY GRAMS (¼ KILO) OF THIS, PLEASE.	Zweihundertfünfzig Gramm (ein Viertel Kilo) davon, bitte. *Tsveye-HOON-dairt-FUHNF-tzikh grahm (eyen FEER-tehl KEE-loh) dah-FON, BITT-tuh.*
MAY I PHOTOGRAPH THIS, PLEASE?	Darf ich das bitte fotografieren? *Dahrf ikh dahs BITT-tuh FOH-toh-grah-FEE-rehn?*

Other Useful Phrases

Sometimes it helps to see in writing a word or phrase that is said to you in German, because certain letters sound distinctly different in English than in German. You may be familiar with the word and its German translation but less familiar with its pronunciation. The following phrase comes in handy if you want to see the word or phrase you are hearing.

PLEASE WRITE IT ON THIS PIECE OF PAPER.

Schreiben Sie das bitte auf diesen Zettel.

SHREYE-behn zee dahs BITT-tuh owf DEE-zehn TSEH-tehl.

Interested in bringing home books about German food?

WHERE CAN I BUY A GERMAN COOKBOOK THAT IS WRITTEN IN ENGLISH?

Wo kann ich ein deutsches Kochbuch, das in englischer Sprache geschrieben ist, kaufen?

Voh kahn ikh eyen DOY-chuh KAWKH-bookh, dahs in EHNG-lish-uh SHPRAH-khuh ges-SHREE-behn ist, KOW-fehn?

And, of course, the following phrases also are useful to know.

WHERE ARE THE RESTROOMS, PLEASE?

Wo sind die Toiletten, bitte?
Voh zint dee toy-LEH-tehn, BITT-tuh?

CHECK, PLEASE.

Die Rechnung, bitte.
Dee REKH-nuhng, BITT-tuh.

DO YOU ACCEPT CREDIT CARDS?

Nehmen Sie Kreditkarten?
NAY-mehn zee kreh-DEET-KAHR-tehn?

Menu Guide

Here is an alphabetical listing of German food preparations, accompanied by English translations. Use the *Menu Guide* as a resource when ordering from a *Speisekarte* (restaurant menu) or making sense of food signs at festivals, outdoor markets, and grocery delicatessens.

Some entries acknowledge the influence that other countries have on Germany's culinary scene, but the primary emphasis is on traditional and regional dishes. The most noteworthy dishes are labeled in page margins as a "national favorite" (popular throughout the country) or "regional classic" (a specialty of a smaller geographic area). We also use the margins to note personal favorites.

Many German and English sources were consulted to compile the *Menu Guide*. The work included interviews with German chefs and tour guides, cookbooks, restaurant menus, books, food articles, and online archives for reputable culture and culinary specialists.

Although many notable food preparations appear on these pages, it is impossible to include all of Germany's bounty. For starters, the country produces more than 1,500 kinds of sausage and at least 500 types of breads! Delicious diversity also exists among German-made beers and wines, many of which are small-batch products with deep loyalty from hometown residents. Within the country are 1,250 breweries and 13 wine-growing regions.

Please be aware that even a national favorite might not taste the same from one part of Germany to the next because of regional twists and creative chefs who love to experiment.

Sauerbraten is one example: The specific sweet–sour flavor of this roast will depend upon the cook and the region in which it is made. Near the Rhine River, for example, fruit (especially raisins) and sugar beet syrup complement the dish's tangy vinegar–wine marinade. Spice combinations and the use of vegetables or crushed gingersnaps (as a gravy thickener) will give the dish distinctly different tastes.

Germans begin the day with *Frühstück,* a breakfast of coffee and a bread or roll that contains cheese, cold cuts, *Leberwurst* (liverwurst), or fruit marmalade.

Heartier eaters add eggs and meat (ham to salami). In Munich, a traditional breakfast means *Weißwurst* (a white veal sausage), warm and fat Bavarian pretzels, and *Weißbier* (wheat beer).

A mid-morning meal of a small sandwich or roll and fruit is the *zweites Frühstück* (second breakfast). *Frühstücksbrettchen* are small boards that sometimes are used, instead of plates, to serve breakfast or a snack.

Mittagessen (lunch) begins at noon and usually is the day's biggest meal. It is not unusual for independently owned businesses to close for an hour or two at this time. Although Germans have long preferred to make lunch a family meal, it is not often practical in contemporary society because of work and school schedules.

Note that *Brotzeit* means "bread time" and refers to a snack between meals. It is similar, in spirit, to an afternoon break for *Kaffee und Kuchen* (coffee and cake) or *Nachmittagstee* (afternoon tea).

Abendessen or *Abdenbrot* (dinner) tends to wind down the day around 7 PM with lighter fare: soup, salad, bread, and sausage or cold cuts with cheese. This is the longstanding tradition, but many restaurants have adapted their menus to provide multiple courses and wide-ranging offerings to match the dining rhythms of international visitors.

Expect food to be served at *Bierhallen* and *Weinstuben* (beer halls and wine bars), as well as the city *Rathskeller* (a restaurant, often below ground, in the town hall) and *Schnellimbiss* (a snack bar or take-away food stall).

For centuries, the *Gasthof*, which signifies the presence of a beer or wine cellar, has fostered casual and friendly gatherings among neighbors and friends. Soft lights, earthenware mugs, and hearty fare are typical. The *Stammtisch,* or friends' table, is for the regular patrons who convene informally and often, after work or church, to enjoy each others' company and catch up on local news. Consider it a predecessor to networking.

The *Eintopf,* in conversation and on menus, refers to one-dish meals that are similar in concept to Midwest casseroles or stews. This is an economical and popular way for families to dine. The long- and slow-simmering dishes are a good way to use leftover fishes and meats, to which vegetables, dumplings or potatoes, spices, and sometimes fruits are added.

When poultry is used, it is as likely to be duck or goose as chicken, especially during the Christmas season, when roasted goose is a longstanding tradition for average German families.

The *süße Speisen* (sweet dishes) that end a meal likely are not as over-sugared as the typical U.S. dessert. Rice puddings, egg custards, cakes, and biscuits are likely to be naturally sweetened with fruit. Refined sugar, although not avoided, is not the predominant draw. The final course is a matter of both artistry and good taste.

The *Sektfrühstück* is a Champagne breakfast during which lobster, caviar, salmon, and foie gras are served. The elegant morning meal historically has been a way for the well-heeled to complete a long and lovely evening of dancing and socializing.

The *Katerfrühstück* is the working person's version of the same thing, a breakfast to ease a hangover. On this table are sausages and ham, pumpernickel bread, goulash soup, and herring in sour cream and dill. To drink? "A hair of whatever dog it was that bit you," explains the late food writer Nika Standen Hazelton, a German diplomat's daughter.

Few Germans call themselves teetotalers. As of 2012, the legal drinking age is 16 for beer and wine; hard liquor cannot be purchased until age 18. Beginning at age 14, it is fine for a teen to drink beer or wine in public, if accompanied by a parent or legal guardian.

Alcoholic beverages are served at snack bars to restaurants. They are sold at newspaper stands and gas stations to food stores and gastropubs. Municipalities determine sales hours, but the lack of limits is not unusual.

Only religion, it seems, has the power to trump drinking traditions. Public parties are illegal nationally on Good Friday, for example, although alcoholic beverages can be sold on that day.

Imbibing is one thing, but driving under the influence of alcohol is quite another. German law enforcers demonstrate low tolerance for drunken driving: First offenders pay a stiff fine and may lose their driver's license. Repeat offenders face a prison sentence. So enjoy yourself but avoid getting behind the wheel afterward.

When dining, advice to *sich verwöhnen lassen* (let yourself be pampered) pops up frequently when Germans talk about food and dining. Let it be this way for the tourist, too! It doesn't matter if you are ordering a *delikate Kleinigkeit* (a delicious little trifle) or an *ausgiebigen Mahlzeit* (hearty meal). Savor it all.

Use this *Menu Guide* in conjunction with the *Foods & Flavors Guide* to explore the hearty cuisine of Germany, food carts to fine dining. When a menu lists a dish that is not included in the *Menu Guide,* look for a translation of key ingredients in *Foods & Flavors.*

When you see *Trinkgeld inklusive* at a restaurant, it means tipping is included with the meal price. When you are ready to leave, ask for *Wechsel oder Scheck* (the bill or check).

REGIONAL CLASSIC **Aachener Printen** gingerbread made with sugar beet syrup instead of honey. A specialty of Aachen.

Aal nach trentiner Art grilled eel.

Aalsuppe eel soup.

REGIONAL CLASSIC **Allgäuer Käsesuppe** a cheese soup from the Alllgäu Alps, home to Germany's densest concentration of dairy cattle.

Allgäuer Nudelgratin pasta casserole with a cheese–wine sauce.

Anisplatzchen anise-flavored cookies.

REGIONAL CLASSIC **Äpfel im Schlafrock** pared, cored apples filled with a mixture of almonds, raisins, and cinnamon sugar, then covered with dough and baked. The name means "apples in nightgowns."

Äpfel, Kirsch, Rhabarber, Stachelbeer Kaltschale a cold fruit soup of apples, cherries, rhubarb, and gooseberries.

Apfelauflauf apple souffle.

Apfelbettelmann stewed apples baked with a mix of grated brown bread, almonds, raisins, and cinnamon sugar. The name means "apple beggar."

DELICIOUS **Apfelkuchen** apple cake.

Apfelkücherl batter-coated apple slices that are deep-fried.

Apfelküchlein apple cookies.

Apfelmus Crème applesauce cream. See recipe, p. 62.

GOOD CHOICE **Apfelpfannkuchen** apple pancakes.

NATIONAL FAVORITE **Apfelrotkohl** apples and red cabbage, marinated in wine and spices, then simmered to soften and thicken. See recipe, p. 60.

Apfelschörle sparkling fruit juice.

VERY POPULAR **Apfelstrudel** apple strudel.

Apfelweinkuchen aus Hessen apple wine cake from Hesse. See recipe, p. 64.

REGIONAL CLASSIC **Appeltaat** a two-crust apple pie and favorite in the Rhineland.

arme Ritter bread slices soaked in milk, eggs, sugar, and vanilla, then pan-fried. It is similar to French toast. The name means "poor knights."

Aspik aspic.

Auberginenragout eggplant ragout, a stew.

aufgeschmalzene Brotsuppe a broth-based soup of dry bread, onions, and seasonings. A specialty of Bavaria.

Auflauf sweet or savory pie, casserole, or soufflé.

Augsburger Reistorte lemon-rich cake, made with rice and baked in a springform pan.

Austern Cocktail oyster cocktail.

Bäckeoffe marinated meats that are braised with root vegetables in a clay pot and covered with a layer of bread dough. See recipe, p. 54.

Bäckerkartoffeln sliced potatoes baked in a cider–cream sauce.

Backesgrumbeere a casserole of sliced potatoes, sour cream, and bacon. It is sometimes seasoned with cinnamon. The casserole originated in southern Germany. REGIONAL CLASSIC

Backhähnchen fried chicken.

badische Zwiebelsuppe creamy onion soup.

Bamberger Krautbraten a meat loaf of ground beef, pork, and cabbage. A Franconia specialty. REGIONAL CLASSIC

Bananensalat chopped banana mixed with a dressing of cream, olive oil, and lemon juice.

Bauernbrot hearty rye–wheat bread with sourdough, known as "farmer's bread." Usually baked in a brick oven.

Bauernfrühstück a mix of potatoes, ham, eggs, and onions that translates as a "farmer's breakfast." GOOD CHOICE

Baumkuchen known as the "king of cakes" because the recipe involves up to 25 thin layers of dough. The hub of production, for centuries, has been Salzwedel in Saxony. NATIONAL FAVORITE

Bautzener Topfsülze cured pork knuckles and pickles in aspic. Served with fried potatoes.

bayerische Crème Bavarian cream, a classic dessert of whipped cream with an egg custard. Used as a cake and pastry filling, but also eaten as a mousse. NATIONAL FAVORITE

bayerische Semmelklösse dumplings made with bread, eggs, and bacon or ham.

bayerisches Gulasch Bavarian goulash. DELICIOUS

bayerisches Kraut sauerkraut that contains apples. VERY POPULAR

Bechamelkartoffeln boiled potatoes tossed with bacon and creamy bechamel sauce. Often served with marinated herring in parts of northern Germany.

Beerdigungskuchen butter cake, often served at funerals (translates as "burial cake"). Also known as *Butterkuchen*.

Beignettenteig a sweet, rum-spiked, flour-based batter for coating and deep-frying pieces of fruit.

bergische Kaffeetafel a special-occasion meal of waffles, sour cherries, honey, and apple purée, plus platters of sausages, ham, and cheeses. Served with coffee. It is popular in parts of western Germany.

Berliner Ballen sweet, fried, yeast doughnut with jam or other filling. Usually they are topped with icing or sugar. Also known REGIONAL CLASSIC as a *berliner Pfannkuchen* or *Krapfen*. They began as a New Year's Eve pastry sold in Berlin; as a joke, you could buy one filled with mustard.

REGIONAL CLASSIC **Berliner Hühnerfrikassee** boiled chicken and asparagus, added to a broth-based sauce that includes sautéed mushrooms.

REGIONAL CLASSIC **Berliner Luft** apple-flavored mousse topped with berries.

REGIONAL CLASSIC **Berliner Pfannkuchen** sweet, fried, yeast doughnut with a filling. Also known as *berliner Ballen* or *Krapfen*.

Berliner Schmorgurken a stew of cucumbers, bacon, and shallots. Tossed with sour cream and dill.

Berliner Weiße mit Schuß wheat beer and raspberry syrup, a Berlin beverage specialty.

Bethmännchen marzipan cookies with almonds. It is a specialty of Frankfurt.

Bettseichersalat dandelion salad, which accompanies potato dishes in Saarland.

Bibbelchesbohnesupp soup with green beans, bacon, and potatoes, popular in Saarland.

GOOD CHOICE **Bienenstich** custard-filled and honey-colored cake.

VERY POPULAR **Bierbrezel** a large, soft, and popular pretzel in Bavaria. Also see *Brezel* and *Laugenbrezel*.

Biersuppe soup of flat beer, citrus, beaten eggs, and cinnamon that is served hot or chilled.

REGIONAL CLASSIC **Birnen, Bohnen, und Speck** pears, green beans, and bacon. Also known as *gröne Hein*. A favorite in northern and central Germany.

Birnen-Eintopf a stew of smoked ham, potatoes, and pears.

Blaubeersuppe blueberry soup, made with red wine, sweetened with cinnamon sugar, and served chilled. Sometimes little, tart bilberries are a substitute for the blueberries.

Bleichsellerie mit Roquefortkäse raw celery topped with a mix of Roquefort cheese and butter.

Blumenkohlsuppe cauliflower soup.

VERY POPULAR **böhmische Knödel** Bohemian dumplings, which are made with flour, eggs, bread, and nutmug.

Bohnenkerne cheese-topped casserole of navy beans, tomatoes, bacon, and onions.

Brägele fried potatoes.

Brandenburger Käsesalat salad of cubed cheese and fruits, especially pears grown near the Havel River, near Berlin.

GOOD CHOICE **Bratapfel** cored and baked apple, filled with raisins and marzipan. Usually a winter treat, served with vanilla custard.

Brathendl grilled chicken.

Brathering fried herring.

Brathuhn a la bonne Femme chicken quarters stewed with potato slices, onion, and peas, then flavored with white wine.

Bratkartoffeln fried potatoes.

Bratwurst in Biersoße sausage served with beer-based sauce that is thickened with gingersnaps. An East German specialty. Also known as *stolzer Heinrich*. **REGIONAL CLASSIC**

braune Kuchen gingerbread cookies with candied fruit and a north German specialty. Usually aged at least two weeks before it is eaten. **REGIONAL CLASSIC**

Brezel pretzel. Types include the *Bierbrezel,* large, soft, and popular in Bavaria. The *Laugenbrezel,* a darker brown in color, is crunchy near the knot. **NATIONAL FAVORITE**

Brötchen plain, white roll. Also known as *Semmel* in Bavaria and *Schrippe* in Berlin.

Bubespitzle potato dough that is shaped like fingers, boiled, and then sautéed. Served in the Baden and Palatinate areas. A similar dish is *Stupperche mit Sauerkraut und Speck* in the Saxon area. **VERY POPULAR**

Buchweizenpfannkuchen buckwheat pancakes with bacon and cold coffee or buttermilk. Popular in Münsterland.

Buchweizentorte cranberry-filled buckwheat cake. Some versions substitute lingonberries.

Bückling whole, smoked herring that are not gutted.

Bücklingbutter butter that contains smoked herring.

Buletten fried and flattened dumplings, made from ground pork, beef, or both in Berlin. Also called *Fleischpflanzerl* in Bavaria and *Frikadellen* elsewhere in Germany. **VERY POPULAR**

Büsumer Krabbenragout a dish of tiny North Sea shrimp and mushrooms, simmered with wine. It is then broiled with cheese and bread crumbs. **DELICIOUS**

Butterbrot sandwich made with bread. Also known as *Stulle* in Berlin.

Butterkuchen butter cake that tastes best when devoured within hours of baking. Also known as *Beerdigungskuchen* (burial cake) because it is often served at funerals.

Buttermilchgetzen Pancakes of potatoes, buttermilk, bacon, onion, and eggs. They originated in Saxony.

Buttermilchsuppe mit Birnen buttermilk soup with poached pears. Served hot or chilled.

REGIONAL CLASSIC **Currywurst** Sliced sausage, doused with a sauce that resembles a spicy ketchup. A popular street food, especially in Berlin. See Currywurst sauce recipe, p. 63.

REGIONAL CLASSIC **Dampfnudel** white bread, steamed and browned on the stovetop in a closed pot. Each egg-sized ball of dough may contain vegetables, a sweet filling of fruit, or no filling. Bottoms are crisp and tops are soft. A traditional dish in southern Germany.

Deutsch-Stil Heringssalat German-style herring salad. See recipe, p. 48.

Dibbelabbes potato hash with bacon, served in Saarland.

Dinkelwaffeln spelt waffles.

Dippehas hare cooked in red wine.

REGIONAL CLASSIC **Döner Kebab** pita bread filled with yogurt sauce, vegetables, and spiced, ground lamb that is shaved while grilling on a vertical spit. Turkish-inspired street food, especially popular in Berlin.

Döppekooche casserole of raw and boiled potatoes, mixed with eggs and sour cream, grated apple, and sliced bacon. Popular in western Germany. *Potthucke* is a variation that excludes the apple and bacon.

Dortmunder Rosenkranz smoked pork sausages and sliced potatoes in a meat broth. *Platten in de Pann,* a similar dish, uses fresh sausages.

NATIONAL FAVORITE **Dresdner Christstollen** an oval, sweet, buttery and yeasty Christmas cake that contains candied fruit and is dusted with powdered sugar. Also known as *Stollen,* this cake originated in Dresden.

Eberswalder Spritzkuchen cruller pastries with lemon frosting.

REGIONAL CLASSIC **Eier in Mostrichsoße** boiled eggs in mustard sauce, typically served with boiled potatoes and salad greens. Popular in Berlin.

Eierauflauf egg pudding.

Eiergrog egg grog, a hot mix of yolks, sugar, rum, and water.

GOOD CHOICE **Eierkuchen** a type of pancake that sometimes contains a sweet filling. Sometimes cut into small pieces and presented as a cluster. Also known as *Flädle* in southern Germany.

Eiersalat egg salad.

Eierstich egg dumplings cooked in a double boiler, then cubed.

eingelegter Kürbis pumpkin chunks that are pickled in a spice-enriched, sweet–sour brine and sealed into jars. A Berlin specialty.

eingemachtes Kalbfleisch sliced veal that is browned, then stewed in water plus peppercorns, white wine, and lemon juice.

Eintopf stew.

Eisbein leg of pork.

Elisenlebkuchen gingerbread made with nut meats instead of flour. A specialty of Nuremberg. See recipe, p. 70.   NATIONAL FAVORITE

Ente mit Sauerkirschen roasted duck with a sauce of tart cherries.

Erbsensuppe mit Grießklößchen pea soup with dumplings made from semolina.

Erdbeerbowle a punch of strawberries, dry white wine, and Champagne. It is served at festivals in Hamburg.   DELICIOUS

Erdbeeren mit Schlagrahm strawberries with whipped cream.

errötendes Mädchen a buttermilk-based mousse with fruit gelatin. The name means "blushing maiden." Served as a summer treat.

Erwes green peas, sautéed and puréed. A Rhineland specialty, by tradition served with pigs' feet.   REGIONAL CLASSIC

falscher Hase multi-spiced meat loaf of ground pork, ground beef, and bacon served as an entrée in Berlin. The name literally means "fake hare."

Finkenwerder Scholle plaice (a type of flounder) and bacon. Sauteed leeks are also sometimes added. Named after an island near Hamburg.   GOOD CHOICE

Fisch a la Créme fish baked in a rich and thick sauce of butter and egg yolks or cream.

Fischkartoffeln marble-sized pieces of raw potatoes that are boiled, coated with butter, and served with fish.

Fischrouladen rolled fish fillets with a stuffing of onion, bacon, pickles, and parsley.

Flädle a type of thin pancake that sometimes contains a sweet filling. Also known as *Eierkuchen*.   GOOD CHOICE

Flädlesuppe clear soup with strips of pancakes or noodles. Popular in Swabia.

Fleeschknepp meatballs made from a mixture of pork and beef. Served with horseradish sauce in southern Germany.   DELICIOUS

Fleischkäse literally, meat cheese: finely ground meat that is baked into a loaf. Also known as *Leberkäse* (liver cheese).

Fleischpflanzerl fried and flattened dumplings, made from ground pork, beef, or both in Bavaria. Also called *Buletten* in Berlin and *Frikadellen* elsewhere in Germany.   VERY POPULAR

Fliederbeersuppe elderberry soup, with apples or plums. Served cold or hot.

Forelle mit Sauerampfersoße baked trout with a sorrel sauce.

Forellen in Weißwein trout steamed in white wine.

Frankfurter Kranz a cake with buttercream filling.

REGIONAL CLASSIC **Franzbrötchen** small, buttery, cinnamon-flavored pastry that resembles a croissant. It sometimes contains chocolate or raisins. A specialty of Hamburg.

REGIONAL CLASSIC **Freude und Leidskuchen** "happiness and sorrow cake," a yeast-dough butter cake, sometimes with a topping of almond slices. Served at funerals and weddings, especially in Westphalia and Bremen. Also called *Zuckerkuchen*.

friesischer Krabbensalat shrimp salad with mixed greens, using tiny North Sea crustaceans.

VERY POPULAR **Frikadellen** fried and flattened dumplings, made from ground pork, beef, or both. Also called *Buletten* in Berlin and *Fleischpflanzerl* in Bavaria.

Früchtebrot fruit bread, usually made with dried pears, and sometimes with rye or sourdough. Also known as *Hutzelbrot* or *Kletzenbrot*.

Gaisburger Marsch potato, beef, and *Spätzle* stew. Popular in Swabia, especially Stuttgart.

VERY POPULAR **Gänsebraten** goose, stuffed with fruit (prunes, apples) and roasted. Popular at Christmas.

Gänseleber Brötchen goose liver canapes.

Gänseleber mit Äpfeln chunks of goose liver fried with chopped onions and apples.

Gänseleber Schnitzel goose liver slices coated with seasoned flour, then fried. Served with a sauce made from pan drippings and Port wine.

gebackener Goldbarschfilet baked golden perch fillets.

gebratene Ente roast duckling.

gebratene Hühnerleber chicken livers fried in bacon fat with slices of onion.

gebratener Hummer fried lobster.

Gefilde dumplings in a creamy bacon gravy, served in Saarland.

Gefügelpastete casserole of ground poultry, an egg–cream sauce, onions, and grated cheese.

gefüllte Eier stuffed eggs. Hard-boiled yolks are mixed with minced ham, onions, and anchovies.

gefüllte Klöße potato dumplings stuffed with ground meat.

gefüllte Pute stuffed turkey.

gefüllte Tauben stuffed pigeons.

gefüllter Krautkopf cabbage leaves stuffed with a mixture of GOOD CHOICE ground meat and rice, simmered in seasoned water, then served with tomato sauce.

gefüllter Paprika green peppers stuffed with a mixture of ground DELICIOUS meat and rice, then topped with tomato sauce.

gefülltes Kalbsbrust roasted veal breast with a seasoned bread stuffing.

gefülltes Kapselbrot a hollowed loaf of dark bread stuffed with an aspic of meats, boiled eggs, cheese, and seasonings.

gegrillt Lachs grilled salmon.

gegrillte Hammelkeule grilled leg of mutton.

gehacktes Rinderschnitzel ground beef patties.

gekochte Eier cooked eggs.

gekochte Kartoffelklöße dumplings made with leftover mashed DELICIOUS potatoes and spiced with nutmeg.

gekochten Steinbutt boiled flounder.

gemischter Braten a roast of pork, veal, and mutton.

Gemüse-Müsli vegetable muesli. See recipe, p. 61.

Gequellde potatoes cooked in their skins.

geräucherter Lachs smoked salmon.

geröstete Austern roasted oysters.

gesulzte Forellen small, cooked trout that, when cooled, are REGIONAL CLASSIC placed atop a firm layer of gelatin that is inside a gelatin mold, then covered with dissolved gelatin and refrigerated. When loosened from the mold, the fish appear to be floating in the gelatin. Served with a remoulade sauce.

Glühwein mulled wine, popular during the Christmas season, NATIONAL FAVORITE especially at *Christkindlmarkts*. See recipe, p. 43.

Gockel in Wein chicken in wine.

Goldbarsch auf badische Art ocean perch baked with capers and tomatoes in a wine sauce.

Goldbroiler grilled chicken, in the former East Germany.

Gräwes sauerkraut boiled in wine, served with mashed potatoes topped with fried bacon and onion.

Griebenschmalz lard with pork cracklings. Used as a savory spread NATIONAL FAVORITE for bread.

Grießnockerlsuppe soothing, broth-based dumpling soup and a favorite in Bavaria.

REGIONAL CLASSIC   **gröne Hein** sweet–sour stew of pears, bacon, and green beans. Also known as *Birnen, Bohnen, und Speck*. A favorite in northern and central Germany.

REGIONAL CLASSIC   **grosser Hans** large, steamed dumpling that contains prunes. Eaten with steamed fruit or smoked pork in northern Germany. Also called *Mehlbeutel*.

grüne Grütze gooseberry fruit pudding.

grüne Kartoffelsuppe potato soup with parsley garnish.

REGIONAL CLASSIC   **grüne Soße** a cold sauce made with at least seven types of herbs, served with boiled or baked potatoes and hard-boiled eggs, as well as with meat and fish dishes. A Frankfurt specialty. See recipe, p. 64.

REGIONAL CLASSIC   **Grünkohl und Pinkel** kale and sausage. A winter specialty of northern Germany.

REGIONAL CLASSIC   **Grünkohleintopf** hearty stew of boiled kale, smoked meats, and sausage. Popular in northern Germany.

Grütze gruel, historically made with coarsely ground grain.

Gugelhupf cake baked in a fluted and round pan that has a hole in its center. Also called *Napfkuchen*.

Gulaschsuppe goulash soup, made with pieces of fried meat and spiced with paprika. It is known as a soup of *Rattenschwanze* (rat tails) in Lower Saxony's Hamelin, home to the legend of the Pied Piper.

Gurkengemüse chopped tomatoes, cucumbers, and dill, sautéed in butter and served with a splash of vinegar or lemon juice.

VERY POPULAR   **Gurkensalat** cucumber salad with vinegar and olive oil or sour cream.

Hackbraten hamburger loaf, similar to American meat loaf, but typically browned in a frying pan before being baked in an oven.

Hackepeter raw, ground pork served on buttered bread in Berlin. Also called *Mett*.

REGIONAL CLASSIC   **halve Hahn** gouda cheese in a rye roll. A Cologne snack.

Hamburger Aalsuppe eel soup that contains dried fruit. A specialty of Hamburg.

Hamburger Krebssuppe crab soup with vegetables.

Hammelfleisch Eintopf lamb stew, seasoned with caraway.

Hammelkoteletts lamb chops.

REGIONAL CLASSIC   **Handkäse mit Musik** pungent cheese, marinated with cider vinegar, oil, and onion. Spread on buttered bread, it is served with apple wine in Frankfurt. See recipe, p. 46.

Hasenpfeffer marinated and well-peppered rabbit.

Hazelnussomelette hazelnut omelet.

Hechtklößchen mit Dillsoße fish dumplings in a dill sauce.

Hefeklöße mit Blaubeertunke puffy, yeast-based dumplings that are served with blueberry sauce. A specialty of Niederlausitz, near Berlin. *GOOD CHOICE*

Hefezopf white, plaited yeast bread that sometimes contains raisins. Also called *Stuten.*

Heidesand cookies flavored with browned butter. Originated in Lüneburger Heide, northeastern Germany.

Heidschnuckenkeule roast leg of lamb and vegetables, using North German sheep. *REGIONAL CLASSIC*

Helgolander Hummersuppe lobster soup. A specialty of Helgoland, a North Sea island.

Heringe Hausfrauenart pickled herring. *VERY POPULAR*

Heringe vom Rost oven-grilled herring.

Heringssalat herring salad with dill pickle slices, sour cream, and pickled herring. Pickled beets are also sometimes included. A Bremen specialty. *REGIONAL CLASSIC*

Heringstoast herring on toast.

Himmel und Erde blood sausage with sliced apples and potatoes. Translates as "heaven and earth." *NATIONAL FAVORITE*

Himmelreich a simmered stew of pork chops and dried fruit that has soaked in water for hours. Also called *schlesisches Himmelreich.* This traditional Silesian dish is popular in eastern Germany. *REGIONAL CLASSIC*

Hirnsuppe brain soup.

Hochzeitssuppe broth-based soup, eaten during a wedding celebration, after the ceremony. Might contain chicken, meatballs, asparagus, noodles, or raisins.

Honigparfait frozen honey custard. Originated with honey from the Black Forest.

Hoppelpoppel leftover meats, cut into thin strips, which are added to a hearty scramble of eggs, potatoes, onions, and spices. A Berlin specialty. *REGIONAL CLASSIC*

Hühner Schnitzel sautéed chicken breast cutlet, served with a wine sauce.

Hühnerfrikassee chicken fricassee.

Hummersandwiches lobster canapes.

Hutzelbrot fruit bread, usually made with dried pears, and sometimes with rye or sourdough. Also known as *Früchtebrot* or *Kletzenbrot.*

MENU GUIDE

GOOD CHOICE **Jäger Eintopf** a stew of beef, potatoes, mushrooms, and onions. The name means "hunter's stew."

REGIONAL CLASSIC **Jägerschnitzel** meat cutlet with mushrooms and cream sauce in western Germany. Not to be confused with an East German creation of the same name, which is made with cooked beef-and-pork sausage, *Jagdwurst,* that is sliced and coated with bread crumbs, fried, and served with noodles and a tomato sauce.

DELICIOUS **Kaiserschmarren** pancake pieces, served on a platter, sprinkled with cinnamon sugar, and accompanied by fruit slices. The name means "scrambled pancakes."

Kalbfleischvögel thin slices of veal that are stewed after being rolled up with a buttery stuffing of anchovies, onion, and parsley. The name means "veal birds."

Kalbsbackerl veal cheeks.

Kalbshaxe roast veal shank. Crisp outside, succulent inside.

REGIONAL CLASSIC **Kalbsleber berliner Art** veal liver with apples and onions.

Kalbsnierenbraten roast loin of veal.

Kalbsvogel sliced veal, rolled and stuffed with chopped egg, bacon, and spinach.

Kalte Ente a chilled punch of dry white wine and Champagne.

Kappes und Grumbeere white cabbage and potatoes, served in Saarland.

REGIONAL CLASSIC **Karamelkartoffeln** caramelized potatoes, roasted, with nutmeg. A specialty of northern Germany.

Kärnersbraten beef rib roast with bread stuffing.

REGIONAL CLASSIC **Karpfen polnisch** carp simmered with spiced cherries and dark beer. Then grated gingerbread, almonds, and raisins are added. The name means "Polish carp." It is also called *Weinachtskarpfen* (Christmas carp).

Kartoffelbuletten potato patties, traditionally served with a dried fruit compote. Originated on Rügen, near Mecklenburg-West Pomerania, and Germany's biggest island.

Kartoffelhörnchen crescent-shaped potato dumplings that are baked. Originated in Thuringia.

NATIONAL FAVORITE **Kartoffelknödel** potato dumplings. See recipe, p. 60.

Kartoffeln in de Schale potatoes "in their jackets," boiled in their skins.

Kartoffelpastetchen mashed potato dough, filled with veal.

NATIONAL FAVORITE **Kartoffelpuffer** potato pancakes. Many regional specialties exist. They are made with grated raw, boiled, or leftover mashed potatoes. Sometimes onions, bacon, or cream are added. Sometimes the finished dish is served with applesauce, other fruits, or savory foods such as fish and meats. Also known as *Reibekuchen.*

Kartoffelpüree mashed potatoes.

Kartoffelsalat potato salad, often made with vinegar and bacon or oil instead of mayonnaise (except in parts of northern Germany). Typically served warm. See recipe, p. 49. **NATIONAL FAVORITE**

Kartoffelsuppe potato soup. See recipe, p. 49.

Käsekuchen cheesecake made with *Quark,* a yogurt-like fresh cheese. Topped with fruit or nuts before baking.

Käseomelette cheese omelet.

Käsepastetchen custard of cheese and sour cream. Typically baked in individual custard cups.

Käsespätzle small dumplings baked with cheese and topped with fried onions. A favorite in Swabia.

Kasseler Rippchen smoked, roasted pork loin. **NATIONAL FAVORITE**

Kastaniensuppe creamy, nutmeg-spiced, chestnut soup.

Kastenpickert potato–yeast bread with raisins.

Kerbelsuppe soup made with chervil leaves.

Kerschdscher potato cubes fried in lard.

Kirschhaltschale cherry soup with dumplings of egg whites and sugary cinnamon. Popular in Hamburg.

Kirschsuppe chilled cherry soup, served as an appetizer, palate cleanser between courses, or a refreshingly light entrée. **NATIONAL FAVORITE**

Klaben rich, yeast-based cake with high fruit content.

Kletzenbrot fruit bread, usually made with dried pears, and sometimes with rye or sourdough. Also called *Früchtebrot* or *Hutzelbrot.*

Kliess mit Birnen yeast dough pie of pears.

Kloppschinken breaded ham slices, a traditional Sunday treat in northern Germany. **REGIONAL CLASSIC**

Kloß dumplings, in northern Germany. Also known as *Knödel* in southern Germany. **VERY POPULAR**

Knödel dumplings, in southern Germany. Also known as *Kloß* in northern Germany. **VERY POPULAR**

Knöpfle firm, irregularly shaped, egg-based pasta.

Kochfisch poached fish.

Kohlrouladen cabbage rolls with meat and onion filling. This East German entrée is also called *thüringer Kohlrouladen.* **REGIONAL CLASSIC**

Kokonussmakronen coconut macaroon cookies. **DELICIOUS**

Kölscher Kaviar Cologne nickname for blood sausage.

Kompott stewed fruit. A cold breakfast dish.

Konfiture jam.

Königinpastetchen pastry pockets filled with chopped chicken, tongue, and mushrooms.

GOOD CHOICE **Königsberger Klopse** meatballs served in a creamy gravy.

Kopfsalat mit Sahnesoße pieces of butterhead lettuce, tossed with lemon cream sauce.

Krabbensuppe cream-based soup with shrimp, typically tiny crustaceans from the North Sea.

REGIONAL CLASSIC **Krapfen** sweet, fried, yeast doughnut with a filling. Also known as *berliner Ballen* or *berliner Pfannkuchen*.

REGIONAL CLASSIC **Krautsalat mit Kümmel und Speck** salad of shredded cabbage and bacon, tossed in a caraway vinaigrette. Popular in Bavaria.

VERY POPULAR **Krautwickerle** cabbage that is stuffed, rolled, and braised. A Franconia specialty.

DELICIOUS **Kroketten** small rolls of mashed potatoes, dipped in egg, then bread crumbs, and fried golden brown.

Kürbispastete deep-dish pie with a layered filling of pumpkin, meat, and cheese.

Kurländer Speckkuchen ham-filled pastry appetizer, named after a peninsula in Latvia but also eaten in eastern Germany.

REGIONAL CLASSIC **Labskaus** a reddish hash of beets, herring, meat, potatoes, and onions. Often topped with a fried egg. A favorite of maritimers in northern Germany.

Landleberwurst liver paté.

Lappenpickert small, grated potato pancakes that are served with sweet or savory foods.

NATIONAL FAVORITE **Laugenbrezel** a dark brown pretzel, crunchy near the knot. Also see *Bierbrezel* and *Brezel*.

Leberkäse literally, liver cheese: finely ground meat that is baked into a loaf. Also known as *Fleischkäse*.

Leberklösschen dumplings made with ground calf's liver.

Leberknödel liver dumpling. Also called *Lewwerknepp*.

GOOD CHOICE **Leberknödelsuppe** liver dumpling soup.

Leberspätzle small dumplings with liver in the dough.

NATIONAL FAVORITE **Lebkuchen** gingerbread, spiced with cloves, nutmeg, and cinnamon. Popular at Christmas.

Leineweber potato pancakes that contain strips of boiled potatoes. Also known as *Pillekauken*.

Leipziger Allerlei morel mushrooms and other spring vegetables in a white cream sauce and crayfish butter. **DELICIOUS**

Leipziger Lerchen a mix of morel mushrooms and other spring vegetables, each type cooked separately, then tossed together with butter. Adaptations include shrimp or crabmeat.

Lendenbraten sirloin roast.

Letscho a spicy mix of tomatoes, onions, and bell peppers. Popular in the former East Germany.

Lewwerknepp liver dumpling. Also called *Leberknödel.*

Linsen mit Spätzle lentils with *Spätzle*, considered the national food of Swabia. It began as food for people who couldn't afford meat. **REGIONAL CLASSIC**

luckeles Käs cottage cheese with caraway and other seasonings.

Lungenhaschee calf lungs, sliced thin, in a sweet–sour sauce.

Markklösschen dumplings made with beef marrow.

Marzipan sugary paste of ground almonds and egg whites, used in baking or to create molded candies. In Lübeck, the country's marzipan capital, rosewater replaces egg whites. **NATIONAL FAVORITE**

Matjes marinated herring, served with onions in a bun and popular in northern Germany. **REGIONAL CLASSIC**

Maultaschen dough stuffed with minced, cooked meat and spinach. Resembles ravioli. A Stuttgart specialty. **REGIONAL CLASSIC**

Meerrettichsauce horseradish sauce. **VERY POPULAR**

Mehlbeutel large, steamed dumpling that contains prunes. Eaten with steamed fruit or smoked pork in northern Germany. Also called *grosser Hans.*

Mehlspeisen sweet and savory dishes that are flour-based and found in southern Germany.

Mehrkornbrot multigrain bread.

Meißner Fummel light, delicate baked goods.

Mett raw, ground pork served on buttered bread in Berlin. Also called *Hackepeter.*

Miesmuscheln in Weinsud blue mussels (the most common mussel in Germany) steamed in wine. Popular in fall and winter, when the mussels are harvested from the North and Baltic seas.

Milchreis cooked rice, simmered with milk and flavored with cinnamon and powdered sugar.

Mohnstriezel bread pudding with poppy seeds. Tastes best if not eaten for a few days after preparation.

Möppkenbrot a loaf of finely ground meat, thickened with blood and rye flour. *Pannhas* is similar, but thickened with buckwheat flour and spiced with cloves and allspice.

Muschelcremesuppe cream of mussel soup.

Napfkuchen cake baked in a fluted and round pan that has a hole in its center. Also called *Gugelhupf.*

DELICIOUS **Nürnberger Elisenlebkuchen** Nuremberg gingerbread, made without flour. See recipe, p. 70.

DELICIOUS **Nürnberger Lebkuchen** Nuremberg gingerbread. See recipe, p. 71.

NATIONAL FAVORITE **Obatzda** a bread spread of Camembert cheese, butter, cream, and various seasonings. See recipe, p. 44.

Obstkuchen cake with fruit mixed into the batter.

Obsttorten cake topped with fruit.

Ochsenmaulsalat pickled tongue salad.

Odenwälder Mostbraten marinated pot roast. See recipe, p. 55.

NATIONAL FAVORITE **Ofenschlüpfer** bread pudding. See recipe, p. 69.

paniert Kotelett pork chop, coated with egg and bread crumbs.

Pannfisch skillet mix of potatoes, fish, bacon, and onions. Beaten eggs and parsley are added at the end.

Pannhas a loaf of finely ground meat, thickened with buckwheat flour, and spiced with cloves and allspice. *Möppkenbrot* is similar, but is made with blood and rye flour, and lacks the spices.

Pellkartoffeln potatoes, especially new and petite, that are boiled in their skins and sometimes peeled before eaten.

GOOD CHOICE **Pfannkuchen** thin pancakes, similar to French crepes. Served as savory main dishes with ground meat, bacon, or cheese—or as desserts, with syrup or jam.

NATIONAL FAVORITE **Pfeffernusse** tiny, clove-flavored cookies popular during the Christmas season. The name means "peppernuts."

REGIONAL CLASSIC **Pfefferpotthast** dark-sauced, beef goulash that originated in western Germany.

Pfeffersteak pepper steak.

Pfitzauf single-serving sized souffles, usually served with fruit. A specialty of Swabia.

Pflanzerl meat burgers. See recipe, p. 58.

Pflaumenkuchen plum cake. Also known as *Zwetschgenkuchen*. See recipe, p. 73.   NATIONAL FAVORITE

Pharisäer a hot beverage of coffee and rum, topped with whipped cream. Long popular in northern Germany.   REGIONAL CLASSIC

Pichelsteiner stew with many types of vegetables and meats.

Pickert a specialty pancake from Westphalia.

Pillekauken potato pancakes that contain strips of boiled potatoes. Also known as *Leineweber*.

Pilzauflauf mit Nudeln casserole of sautéed mushrooms and noodles. Sometimes sauerkraut is added.

Pilze im Glas mushrooms baked on toasted, seasoned bread and topped with a creamy, sherry-spiked sauce.

Pilzrahmsauce mushroom cream sauce.

Pinkel small, smoked sausages made with oats and served with kale.   REGIONAL CLASSIC

Platten in de Pann fresh pork sausages and sliced potatoes in a meat broth. *Dortmunder Rosenkranz,* a similar dish, uses smoked sausages.

Plettenpudding fruit-layered pound cake, served as dessert in Thomas Mann's book *Buddenbrooks*. Mann won the 1929 Nobel Prize for Literature.

Plinsen small flour and yeast pancakes, eaten with fruit.

Plockfinken pieces of boiled and cured meats, carrots, onions, and apples in a white roux. Seasoned with vinegar and sugar.

Pommes rot/weiß French fries with ketchup (*rot,* "red") or mayonnaise (*weiß,* "white").

Potthast stew of beef and onions.

Potthucke casserole of raw and boiled potatoes, mixed with eggs and sour cream. Popular in western Germany. *Döppekooche* is a variation that adds grated apple and sliced bacon.   REGIONAL CLASSIC

Prinzregententorte chocolate cake with seven layers, created in 1886 as a tribute to the former kingdom of Bavaria.

Pumpernickel a dark, slow-baked bread invented in Westphalia.   NATIONAL FAVORITE

Quarkkäulchen potato pancakes made with fresh cheese. See recipe, p. 62.

Radler a mix of beer and citrus soda. Originated in Bavaria.   NATIONAL FAVORITE

Rehfilet vom Grill grilled venison fillets.

Rehschnitzel venison cutlets, sometimes simmered with tomatoes, onions, and red wine.

NATIONAL FAVORITE **Reibekuchen** potato pancakes. Also known as *Kartoffelpuffer*.

Reiberdatschi pancakes made with grated raw potatoes and savory seasonings. A specialty of Munich.

Reisschmarren pancakes made with cooked rice, almonds, raisins, and currants.

Rettichsalat white radish salad.

Rhabarbergrütze rhubarb pudding.

REGIONAL CLASSIC **rheinischer Heringsstipp** herring salad with pickles and apples.

REGIONAL CLASSIC **rheinischer Sauerbraten** marinated roast beef, served with a gravy thickened by gingersnaps. The dish is topped with sour cream, raisins, and almonds.

Rievkooche grated potato cakes (similar to potato pancakes), a popular street food in the Rhineland.

Rindergulasch beef goulash.

NATIONAL FAVORITE **Rinderrouladen** pickles, bacon, and onions wrapped in thinly sliced beef before browning and simmering. Also simply known as *Rouladen*.

Ritter Schnitzel sautéed cutlets of pork tenderloin, topped with mushroom sauce.

Roggenbrot rye bread.

Roggenmischbrot rye and wheat bread.

Rohrnudeln baked dumplings, found in southern Germany.

REGIONAL CLASSIC **Rollmopse** fillet of pickled herring that is rolled around a pickle or piece of onion.

Rostbraten roast beef.

rote Bete Salat salad of red beets; some versions contain grated sour apple.

REGIONAL CLASSIC **rote Bete Suppe** beet soup. See recipe for beet soup with horseradish and scallops, p. 52.

NATIONAL FAVORITE **rote Grütze** red fruit pudding, typically made with berries and juice thickened by cornstarch. Usually served with cream, but variations include ice cream, whipped cream, milk, and vanilla sauce.

NATIONAL FAVORITE **Rotkraut** spiced apples and red cabbage.

Rotweinbraten beef braised in red wine.

REGIONAL CLASSIC **Rotweinsuppe** red wine soup, a mix of meat broth, wine, citrus fruit, and spices. It is finished off with a quick whisk of cream. The soup, which originated in eastern Germany, is usually served for breakfast.

Rouladen pickles, bacon, and onions wrapped in thinly sliced NATIONAL FAVORITE
beef, which is browned and simmered. See recipe, p. 57.

Rubenmalheur turnip stew, a Schleswig-Holstein specialty.

Rubenmus mashed turnips.

Rübstiel vegetable dish made with chopped turnip greens that is
popular in Rhineland. Also called *Stielmus.*

Rüdesheimer Kaffee brandy-spiked coffee, topped with whipped DELICIOUS
cream. Invented at the Asbach Distillery in 1957.

Rührei mit Krabben scrambled eggs with shrimp.

Rühreier scrambled eggs.

Rumtopf fruit marinated for months in rum and sugar. It is used REGIONAL CLASSIC
as an ice cream topping or with Bavarian cream. *Rumtopf*
originated in Schleswig-Holstein, Germany's "rum country."

russische Heringsbrötchen Russian herring canapes.

Sachertorte chocolate apricot cake. GOOD CHOICE

sächsisches Zwiebelfleisch tender meat that swims in a gravy REGIONAL CLASSIC
thickened with bread crumbs. Served with potato dumplings.
Comfort food from Saxony.

Salbeiküchle sage leaves, dipped in batter and deep-fried. A Swabian REGIONAL CLASSIC
specialty, served as an appetizer or (with fruit compote) dessert.

Salzkartoffeln potatoes boiled in salted water.

Sardellenbutter butter blended with boned, chopped anchovies.

Sauerbraten meat (usually beef or venison) that is marinated in NATIONAL FAVORITE
vinegar and/or wine (plus spices) for days before roasting.
Typically served with cooked red cabbage.

Sauerfleisch marinated meat.

Sauerkrauteintopf sauerkraut stew.

Sauerkrautsuppe sauerkraut soup. See recipe, p. 50.

Saumagen ground meat and vegetables simmered slow and long GOOD CHOICE
in a pig stomach.

saure Leber und Nieren sliced lamb kidneys and calf's liver fried
with onions in butter, then simmered with vinegar, water,
and seasonings.

saure Rippchen sweet-and-sour pork ribs. It is a specialty of
Schleswig-Holstein.

Schabefleisch lean beef, finely ground and mixed with an egg
yolk, onions, salt, and pepper. Served raw.

Schaschlik skewer of pork, bell pepper, and onion. Sometimes
sold as a fast-food item.

Schinkenpastete pastry dough filled with pork and veal.

Schlachteplatte sauerkraut with meat garnishes that include sausages and cured pork. Served with boiled potatoes.

Schleie mit Sahnemeerrettich carp served with creamed horseradish.

Schleizer Bambser a noodle casserole with apples, eggs, cooked potatoes, sugar, and cinnamon. A specialty of Thuringia.

schlesisches Himmelreich stew of dried fruit and cured pork, a 50–50 mix that is served hot.

Schmalz lard-based bread spread, which also may contain fried apples and onions.

Schmorbraten pot roast.

Schmorgurken cucumber stew.

Schneeballen fried, yeasty pastries that are bumpy in appearance and nicknamed "snowballs." A Rothenburg specialty.

Schnitzel a meat cutlet, typically veal (see *wiener Schnitzel*), coated with bread crumbs and fried.

Schnüsch milk-based vegetable stew, sweetened with milk.

Schokoladeflammeri chocolate pudding.

Schrippe a plain, white roll in Berlin. Also known as *Semmel* in Bavaria and *Brötchen* elsewhere.

Schupfnudeln noodles made with mashed potatoes, similar to Italian gnocchi. Served with goulash as a main dish with sauerkraut, or as a dessert, with a sprinkling of cinnamon and sugar.

schwarz Kirschsuppe black cherry soup, served between courses, to cleanse the palate, or as an appetizer or dessert. See recipe, p. 53.

Schwarzwälder Kirschtorte layers of chocolate cake with whipped cream, sour cherries, and chocolate shavings. Spiked with cherry schnapps. See recipe, p. 65.

Schwarzwaldforelle Black Forest trout.

Schweinebraten pork loin.

Schweinefilet pork fillet. See recipe for pork fillet with apple wine, colorful vegetables, and potatoes, p. 56.

Schweinehaxe pork shank.

Schweinekoteletten mit gebratenen Äpfeln pork chops fried in butter with apple slices.

Schweinelendchen und Pfeffer-Sahnesauce pork tips in a peppery cream sauce.

Schweinerouladen slices of pork rolled up with a stuffing of bread, ground pork, onions, and seasonings, fried, then simmered in stock or water.

Schweinsbraten slow-roasted pork. Typically served with sauerkraut.

Schwemmklösschen dumplings made with flour.

Schwenkbraten marinated pork cutlets, grilled on hot coals. A summer favorite in Saarland.

Seemannslabskaus corned beef and mashed potatoes with fried egg, pickled herring, beetroot, and dill gherkin. A version of *Labskaus* that is a Bremen specialty.

Seezunge in Weisswein sole steamed in white wine.

Semmel a plain, white roll in Bavaria. Also known as *Schrippe* in Berlin and *Brötchen* elsewhere.

Semmelknödel bread dumpling.

Senfbutter a mix of butter, prepared mustard, and mashed, hard-boiled egg yolk.

Serbska Kwasna Poliwka Sorbian wedding soup, a broth with liver dumplings, vegetables, and (occasionally) pasta. See recipe, p. 51. **REGIONAL CLASSIC**

Soljanka East German soup with Russian origins that is spicy and sour. It includes meat or fish, pickled cucumbers, broth, and dill. **REGIONAL CLASSIC**

Spaghettieis an ice cream dessert resembling spaghetti.

Spanferkel a whole suckling pig that is spit-roasted. **NATIONAL FAVORITE**

Spargelfest Salat grilled asparagus and beet salad with honey mustard. See recipe, p. 47.

Spargelsuppe asparagus soup.

Spätzle tiny, irregularly shaped dumplings that also are referred to as noodles. A basic, from-scratch starch, especially good for soaking up rich gravies and sauces. Some versions are fried briefly after boiling. See recipe, p. 59. **NATIONAL FAVORITE**

Spiegeleier sunny-side-up eggs.

Spinatpfannkuchen pancakes that contain spinach.

Sprotten smoked sprats. A fish specialty of Kiel. **REGIONAL CLASSIC**

Stielmus vegetable dish made with chopped turnip greens that is popular in Rhineland. Also called *Rübstiel.*

Stollen an oval, sweet, buttery and yeasty Christmas cake that contains candied fruit and is dusted with powdered sugar. Also known as *dresdner Christstollen* because of its origins in Dresden. **NATIONAL FAVORITE**

stolzer Heinrich sausage served with beer-based sauce that is thickened with gingersnaps. An East German specialty. Also known as *Bratwurst in Biersoße.* **REGIONAL CLASSIC**

strammer Max hearty sandwich of ham and fried eggs. Served open-faced.

Streuselkuchen yeast-dough crumb cake, sometimes filled with fruit or a vanilla cream.

Stulle sandwich, made with bread in Berlin. Also known as *Butterbrot.*

VERY POPULAR **Stupperche mit Sauerkraut und Speck** finger-sized potato dumplings served with sauerkraut and bacon in the Saxon area. A similar dish is *Bubespitzle* in the Baden and Palatinate areas.

Stuten white, plaited yeast bread that sometimes contains raisins. Also called *Hefezopf.*

Sülze head cheese; meat from the head of a pig or calf preserved in aspic.

Suppengrün literally, soup greens: a mix of carrots, celeriac, leeks, parsley root, and fresh parsley.

schwabische Saitenwürstle sausage cooked with lentils and *Spätzle.* A speciality of Swabia.

Sylter Austern broiled oysters.

Sylter Welle spiced red-wine punch. Originated on Sylt, a North Sea island.

NATIONAL FAVORITE **Tafelspitz** boiled beef, usually simmered with root vegetables and spices. Served with potatoes, applesauce, and horseradish sauce.

GOOD CHOICE **Tartar von der buhlbacher Forelle** trout tartare. See recipe for trout tartare with apples and horseradish, p. 45.

Teltower Rübchen white turnips simmered and glazed with a sugar–butter broth. The dish is a tribute to turnips grown near Berlin.

Teufelstomaten butter-fried tomato slices that are topped with a sauce made with butter, egg, sugar, and vinegar. The name means "devil's tomatoes."

Thunfischsteak mit Vinaigrette tuna steak with vinaigrette.

REGIONAL CLASSIC **Thüringer Kloße** crouton-filled dumplings that are a mix of raw and boiled potatoes.

REGIONAL CLASSIC **Thüringer Kohlrouladen** blanched cabbage leaves filled with ground meat, then rolled and simmered in broth. Also known simply as *Kohlrouladen.*

REGIONAL CLASSIC **Thüringer Schnipelsuppe** hearty, broth-based soup of root and other vegetables, plus sliced sausages or frankfurters.

Topfenknödel dessert dumplings made with *Quark* cheese.

NATIONAL FAVORITE **Torte** a popular dessert, which is usually round, layered, and more extravagant than *Kuchen.*

REGIONAL CLASSIC **Töttchen** a sweet–sour ragout of veal, formerly a meal for the poor because it was made with tongue, heart, and other inner organs. A Münster specialty.

Tunke gravy or sauce.

Vanillekipferl vanilla, crescent-shaped cookies. See recipe, p. 68.   NATIONAL FAVORITE

Vollkornbrot whole-grain bread.

Weckklößchen dumplings made with bread.

Weinachtskarpfen "Christmas carp." Carp simmered with spiced cherries and dark beer. Then grated gingerbread, almonds, and raisins are added. Also called *Karpfen polnisch*.

Weinkaltschale chilled soup of wine, citrus, eggs, sugar, and raisins.

Weinkraut sauerkraut with apples and dry white wine.

Weinschorle a mix of wine and soda water.

Weißbrot white bread.

weiße Bohnensuppe white bean soup.

weißem Heringssalat white herring salad.

Weißkraut mit Speck cooked cabbage, potatoes, bacon, and onions.   VERY POPULAR

Weizenmischbrot wheat and rye bread.

Welfenspeise custard–mousse dessert, served at weddings and   GOOD CHOICE
named after the medieval Welfen dynasty.

westfälische Speise dessert made with pumpernickel cubes, tart cherries, and whipped cream.

Wickelklöße potato dough, rolled and stuffed with a bacon   REGIONAL CLASSIC
stuffing. It is a Saxon specialty.

Wiener Schnitzel thin slices of veal cutlets that are coated with   NATIONAL FAVORITE
bread crumbs and fried. See recipe, p. 57.

Wintereintopf a stew of sausage, turnips, chestnuts, and leeks.

Winterkohl cooked cabbage that is harvested after the first frost of the season.

Wurstebrei gruel-like mix of pearl barley with ground pork and pork heart.

Wurstsalat salad of sausage, onions, vinegar, oil, and sometimes   REGIONAL CLASSIC
cheese, which originated in Bavaria.

Wurzelfleisch stew of sliced beef and root vegetables, as prepared in Saxony-Anhalt.

Ziegeunerschnitzel pork tenderloin cutlet, fried with tomatoes, green peppers, and a paprika sauce. "*Ziegeuner*" refers to gypsies.

Zimtsterne star-shaped almond cookies, flavored with cinnamon.   NATIONAL FAVORITE
They are glazed with sweetened egg whites. See recipe, p. 67.

Zitronencreme lemon mousse, a treat usually reserved for weddings   GOOD CHOICE
and holidays.

REGIONAL CLASSIC   **Zuckerkuchen** yeast-dough butter cake, sometimes with a topping of almond slices. Served at funerals and weddings, especially in Westphalia and Bremen. It is also known as the *Freude und Leidskuchen* (happiness and sorrow) cake.

Zwetschgenknödel dumplings that contain mashed potatoes and a plum filling.

REGIONAL CLASSIC   **Zwetschgenkuchen** plum-topped yeast sheet cake and a specialty of Augsburg.

Zwetschgenpavesen French toast filled with puréed prunes. Eaten hot or cold.

Zwiebelbrot bread with roasted onions.

NATIONAL FAVORITE   **Zwiebelkuchen** onion cake. It is especially popular in wine regions in autumn.

REGIONAL CLASSIC   **Zwiebel-Speck-Kuchen** onion-filled quiche, especially popular during Weimar's annual Onion Market.

Foods & Flavors Guide

Consult this list when deciphering a German menu or recipe, or exploring the country's shops and markets. Pertinent foods, spices, kitchen equipment, and cooking terminology are presented alphabetically in German, then translated into English.

Germany produces many types of sausages; this guide lists some of the most common varieties.

The "ß" is treated as "ss" when alphabetizing, and the vowels with umlauts are alphabetized with their base letters (*Ähre*, for example, comes before *alkoholfrei*). Nouns are capitalized. Not included are German words that are the same, or nearly the same, as the English translation.

If you are intrigued with an item that is not identified by signage, ask "*Wie heißt das?*" ("What is this called?") or use the *Helpful Phrases* section of this book for additional ways to converse about food.

Aal eel.

Abendbrot supper.

Abendessen dinner, referring to the evening meal.

abgestanden stale, as in flat beer.

abmessen measure.

Ackergauchheil pimpernel, a flowered plant (*Anagallis tenella*) of the primrose family, used in sauces.

Ahornsirup maple syrup.

Ahornzucker maple sugar.

Ähre ear of corn.

alkoholfrei non-alcoholic.

Ananas pineapple.

Apfel apple.

Apfelessig cider vinegar.

Apfelkraut apple butter.

Apfelkuchen apple cake.

Apfelmus applesauce.

Apfelsaft apple juice.

Apfelschorle apple spritzer.

Apfelwein apple wine made from cider, served sweet, sour, or straight-up. A specialty in and near Frankfurt.

Aprikose apricot.

Artischocken artichoke.

Artischockenherz artichoke heart.

Äsche grayling (*Thymallus thymallus*), a fish in the salmon family.

atlantischer Heilbutt Atlantic halibut (*Hippoglossus hippoglossus*).

Aubergine eggplant.

Auflauf casserole, soufflé.

Aufschnitt cold cuts.

Auster oyster (*Ostrea edulis*).

Bachsaibling brook trout or char (*Salvelinus fontinalis*); also called *Saibling*.

Bäcker baker.

Bäckerei bakery.

Backpulver baking powder.

Baiser meringue.

Banane banana.

Basilikum basil.

Bedienung und Mehrwertsteuer inklusiv service and value-added tax included.

Beere berry.

Bein leg.

Beiz pub. Also called *Kneipe*.

Berg Johannisbeere mountain currant (*Ribes alinum*), a small, juicy berry resembling a red currant.

Bergseeforelle mountain lake trout.

Besteck flatware, silverware.

Bier beer.

Bierkrug beer stein.

Bierwurst pork–beef sausage, with mustard seed and garlic, served sliced as a cold cut.

Bioladen store with organic foods. Also called *Ökoladen*.

Birkhuhn black grouse.

Birne pear.

Birnendicksaft concentrated pear juice.

Bissen Nahrung morsel of food.

Blätterteig puff pastry.

Blattsalat leaf lettuce.

Blaubeere blueberry.

Blauschimmelkäse blue cheese.

Blumenkohl cauliflower.

Blut blood.

blutig rare (as in undercooked meat).

Blutwurst blood sausage, also known as blood pudding or black pudding, served as a sliced cold cut or eaten hot as cooked links.

Bockshornklee fenugreek (*Trigonella foenum-graecum*); leaves and seeds are used for flavoring.

Bockwurst veal-pork sausage, eaten hot as cooked links, traditionally served with bock beer.

Bohne bean; string bean.

Bohnensprossen bean sprouts.

Borretsch borage, an herb with cucumber-like flavor, used in preparation from salads to sauces.

Brasse bream (*Abramis ballerus*).

Braten roast (as in cut of meat).

Brauerei brewery. Also called *Brauhaus*.

Brauhaus brewery. Also called *Brauerei*.

brauner Zucker brown sugar.

Braunschweiger a finely ground pork-liver sausage, served as a sandwich or paté spread. A more generic term for liver sausage is *Leberwurst*.

breitblättrige Endivie broad-leaved endive or escarole (*Cichorium endivia var. latifolia*).

Brezel pretzel.

Brokkoli broccoli.

Brombeere blackberry or brambleberry (*Rubus fructicosus*).

Brot bread.

Brötchen roll.

Brotlaib loaf of bread.

Brotscheibe slice of bread.

Brühe broth; soup stock.

Brunnenkresse watercress.

Brust breast.

Büchsenöffner can opener.

Buchweizen buckwheat.

Bulette meatball.

Cambozola soft, blue-veined German cheese.
Cashewnüss cashew nut.
Cayennepfeffer cayenne pepper.
Champignon white button mushroom (*Agaricus brunnescens*).
Country-Stil country style.
Cremesuppe cream soup.

Dattel date
destilliert distilled.
Dillsamen dill seed.
Dörrobst dried fruit.
Dotter egg yolk.

Ei egg.
Eichblattsalat oakleaf lettuce (*Lactuca sativa crispa*), a type of loose-leaf lettuce available in red and green varieties.
Eierbecher egg cup.
Eigelb egg yolk.
eingelegter Hering pickled herring.
Einkaufskorb shopping basket.
Eintopf stew.
Eis ice; also means ice cream.
Eisbergsalat iceberg lettuce.
Eistee iced tea.
Eiswasser ice water.
Eiweiß egg white.
Elch moose; European elk (*Alces alces*).
Ente duck.
Erbse pea.
Erdapfel potato ("apple of the earth"). Also called *Kartoffel*.
Erdbeere strawberry.
Erdnuss peanut.
Erdnussbutter peanut butter.
Erdnussöl peanut oil.
essen eat.
Essen food.

Essig vinegar.

Essiggurke pickle.

Estragon tarragon.

europäische Ensis European razor clam (*Solen vagina*).

europäische Scholle European plaice (*Pleuronectes platessa*), a flatfish with smooth, brown skin and small, reddish-orange spots.

europäische Seehecht European hake (*Merluccius merluccius*), a member of the cod family.

europäische Sprotte European sprat (*Sprattus sprattus*), a member of the herring family.

Fassbier draft beer. Also called *Schankbier*.

Favabohne fava bean.

Feige fig.

Fenchel fennel.

fettarme Milch low-fat milk.

Fettglasur icing or glaze.

Filo-Teig phyllo pastry dough.

Fisch fish.

Fischgerichte fish dishes, a term seen as a header on menus.

Fischrogen fish roe.

Fitnessbrot rye, oat, and wheat-germ bread.

Fladenbrot flatbread or crispbread. Also known as *Knäckebrot*.

Flasche bottle.

Flaschenbier bottled beer.

Fleisch meat.

Fleischbrühe meat bouillon.

Fleischgerichte meat dishes, a term seen as a header on menus.

Fleischwolf food grinder.

Flunder European flounder (*Platichthys flesus*).

Flussbarsch European perch (*Perca fluviatilis*).

Flusskrebs crayfish or crawfish; also called *Languste* or *Süßwasserkrebse*.

Forelle trout.

Frankfurter small sausages that are slightly smoked. They can be made with beef, pork, or poultry. Also called *Wiener, Würstchen, Halberstädter* in Thuringia, *Schübling* in Swabia, and *Rindswürstchen* when made with beef in Frankfurt.

Freilandeier free-range eggs.

Frikadelle meatball.
frisch fresh.
Frischkäse fresh or cream cheese.
Frisee curly endive or chicory (*Cichorium endivia var. cirspum*).
frittiert deep-fried.
Froschschenkel frog's legs.
Frucht fruit. Also known as *Obst*.
Fruchtsaft fruit juice.
Frühlingszwiebel spring onion or scallion; also called *Lauch*.
Frühstück breakfast.
Frühstücksbrettchen small boards, sometimes used instead of plates for serving breakfast or a snack.
Füllung filling or stuffing.

Gabel fork.
Gans goose.
Gartenbohne kidney bean.
Gartenminze garden mint.
Gebäck pastry.
gebeizt sour; pickled. Another word for *gebeizt* is *sauer*.
gedünstet steamed.
Geflügel poultry.
Geflügelgerichte poultry dishes, a term seen as a header on menus.
geheilt Fisch cured (salted and dried) fish.
geheilt Fleisch cured (salted and dried) meat.
geheilt Schinken cured (salted and dried) ham.
geheilt Speck cured (salted and dried) bacon.
Gehirn brain.
Geiß goat. Also known as *Ziege*.
gekocht boiled.
gelbe Bergplaume plum schnapps.
gelbe Erbsen yellow pea.
gelbe Zwiebel yellow onion.
Gelbwurst yellow veal sausage, flavored with ginger and nutmeg or with parsley and lemon; served sliced as a cold cut.
Geldschein bill of money, currency.
Gelee jelly.
gemahlen ground.

Gemüse vegetable.
Gemüsemarkt vegetable market.
Gemüsesaft vegetable juice.
geräucherte Heringe smoked herring.
geräucherte Wurst smoked sausage.
geräucherten Fisch smoked fish.
geräucherter Schinken smoked ham.
gerieben grated.
geriebene Semmel bread crumbs. Also known as *Paniermehl*.
geröstet roasted.
Gerste barley.
Gerstenmehl barley flour.
Geschirrtuch dish towel.
geschmort braised.
geschreddert shredded.
getoastet toasted.
Getränk beverage.
Getreide cereal.
getrocknet dried.
Gewürze spices.
Gewürznelken cloves.
Granatapfel pomegranate.
Graubrot rye-wheat sourdough bread.
Graupen pearl barley.
Grieß semolina.
grillen grill; broil.
Grobeleberwurst coarsely ground liver sausage, served as a sliced cold cut.
große Jakobsmuschel king scallop, great scallop, or Saint-Jacques scallop (*Pecten maximus*); also called *König Jakobsmuschel*.
grüne Bohne green bean.
grüne Pfeffer green pepper.
grüne Soße a cold sauce made with at least seven types of herbs, served with boiled or baked potatoes and hard-boiled eggs, as well as with meat and fish dishes.
Grüneminze spearmint.
Grünkohl kale.
Grütze fruit jelly.
günstig cheap, inexpensive.
Gurke cucumber; gherkin; pickle.

hacken chop.

Hackfleisch ground meat.

Hafer oats.

Haferbrei porridge.

Haferflocken rolled oats; oat groats.

Hafermehl oat flour.

Haferschleim gruel; thin cooked cereal.

Hähnchen chicken.

Halberstädter small sausages that are slightly smoked in Thuringia. They can be made with beef, pork, or poultry. Also called *Frankfurter, Wiener, Würstchen, Schübling* in Swabia, and *Rindswürstchen* when made with beef in Frankfurt.

Hammelfleisch mutton.

harte Walze hard roll.

hartgekocht hard-boiled.

hartgekochtes Ei hard-boiled egg.

Hartweizen durum wheat.

Hartweizenmehl durum wheat flour.

Hase hare.

Haselhuhn hazel hen or hazel grouse (*Tetrastes bonasia*).

Haselnuss hazelnut.

Hauptgericht main dish.

Hauptspeise main course.

Haus Spezialität house specialty.

hausgemacht homemade.

Hecht northern pike (*Esox lucius*).

Hefe yeast.

Hefeweizen wheat beer.

Heidelbeere blueberry (*Vaccinium corymbosum*).

Heilbutt halibut.

heiße Schokolade hot chocolate; cocoa.

helles Bier light beer; pale ale.

Henne hen; chicken. Refers to the animal, not the meat, which is *Geflügel*.

herb dry, as in wine.

Herz heart.

Himbeere raspberry (*Rubis ideaus*).

Hirschfleisch venison.

Hirse millet.

Holunderbeere elderberry.

Honig honey.
Honigmelone honeydew melon.
Hopfen hops.
Hühnerbrühe chicken bouillon.
Hühnerbrüst chicken breast.
Hühnersuppe chicken soup.
Hummer lobster (*Homarus gammarus*).
Hüttenkäse cottage cheese.

Imbiss snack.
Imbissbude snack bar.
Ingwer ginger.
Innereien offal; variety meats.
Instant-Kaffee instant coffee.

Jakobsmuschel scallop.
Joghurt yogurt.
Johannisbeere currant.

Kabeljau cod.
Kaffee coffee.
Kaffee mit Sahne coffee with cream.
Kaiser Messbecher Kayser measuring cup, an all-in-one kitchen tool that measures liters, milliliters, grams, cups, and ounces. It has separate grids for measuring sugar, flour, cereal, and rice.
Kakao cocoa.
Kalbfleisch veal.
Kalbsbries sweetbreads.
Kalbsfilet fillet of veal.
Kalbsleber calf's liver.
Kalbsschnitzel veal cutlet.
kalte cold.
Kamillentee chamomile tea.
kandierte candied.
Kaninchen rabbit.
Karotte carrot.

Karpfen European carp (*Cyprinus carpio*).

Kartoffel potato. Also called *Erdapfel* ("apple of the earth").

Kartoffelbrei mashed potato. Also called *Kartoffelpüree*.

Kartoffelknödel potato dumpling.

Kartoffelmehl potato flour.

Kartoffelpüree mashed potato. Also called *Kartoffelbrei*.

Kartoffelsalat potato salad.

Käse cheese.

Käse Ebene cheese plane.

Käsebrot open-faced cheese sandwich.

Kassler Rippchen smoked pork chops.

Kastanie chestnut.

Kastenkuchen loaf cake.

Keks biscuit.

Kellner waiter; waitress is *Kellnerin*.

Kellnerin waitress; waiter is *Kellner*.

Kerbel chervil.

Kichererbse chickpea or garbanzo bean.

Kinder-Menü children's menu.

Kirsche cherry.

Kirschwasser cherry-flavored schnapps.

Kleie bran.

kleinen Maräne vendace (*Coregonus albulathe*), the European whitefish.

Knäckebrot flatbread or crispbread. Also known as *Fladenbrot*.

knackig crisp.

Knackwurst pinkish beef-pork sausage, eaten hot as cooked links.

Kneipe pub. Also called *Beiz*.

Knoblauch garlic.

Knochen bone.

Knödel dumpling.

Koch chef, cook.

kochen Apfel cooking apple.

Kochkäse a popular cooked cheese spread for crackers or bread.

Kochkunst cuisine.

koffeinfrei decaffeinated.

Kohl cabbage.

Kokosnuss coconut.

Konditorei pastry shop.

Konfitür jam.

König Jakobsmuschel king scallop, great scallop, or Saint-Jacques scallop (*Pecten maximus*); also called *große Jakobsmuschel*.

Königskrabbe red king crab.

Königskuchen a narrow loaf pan, about 12 inches long, used for pound cakes and other baking.

Konserven canned goods; preserves.

konzentrierten Saft concentrated juice, which must be diluted before drinking.

Kopfsalat head lettuce.

Korkenzieher corkscrew.

Kotelett pork chop.

Krake octopus.

Kräutertee herbal tea.

Krautsalat coleslaw.

Kren horseradish. Also called *Meerrettich*.

Kresse garden cress.

Kreuzkümmel cumin.

Kristallzucker granulated sugar.

Krokette croquette.

Kuchen cake.

Kuh cow.

Kümmel caraway.

Kürbis pumpkin.

Kürbis-Marmelade pumpkin marmalade.

Kurkuma tumeric.

Lachs salmon.

Laib Brot loaf of bread.

laichen Kabeljau spawning codfish.

Lamm lamb.

Landjäger semi-dried beef-pork sausage, eaten as a cold, chewy snack link.

Languste crayfish or crawfish; also called *Flusskrebs* or *Süßwasserkrebse*.

Lattich romaine lettuce or cos lettuce; also called *Römersalat*.

Lauch spring onion, leek, or scallion; also called *Frühlingszwiebel*.

Laugenbrötchen pretzel roll.

Lebensmittel groceries.

Lebensmittelgeschäft grocery store.

Leber liver.

Leberkäse liver cheese.

Leberpastete liver paté.

Leberwurst liver sausage, served as a cold cut or, when finely ground, spread as a paté. Also known as *Braunschweiger* when pork liver is used.

Lebkuchen gingerbread.

leicht gebraten lightly grilled.

leicht gekocht lightly cooked.

Leinsamen flaxseed.

Lendenfilet sirloin.

Liebstöckel lovage, a spicy herb used sparingly in soups to casseroles.

Likör liqueur.

Limabohne lima bean.

Linsensuppe lentil soup.

Löffel spoon.

Lorbeerblatt bay leaf.

Löwenzahn dandelion.

Magermilch skim milk.

Mahlzeit meal.

Mais corn.

Maismehl cornmeal; corn flour.

Maisöl corn oil.

Majoran marjoram.

Makrele Atlantic mackerel (*Scomber scombrus*).

Malzbier malt beer.

Mandel almond.

Mandelöl almond oil.

Mangold Swiss chard.

mariniert marinated.

Marzipan almond paste.

Matjes marinated herring, served with onions in a bun and popular in northern Germany.

Maulbeere mulberry.

Meer Jakobsmuschel sea scallops.

Meerforelle sea trout; brown trout (*Salmo trutta*).

Meerrettich horseradish. Also called *Kren*.

Mehl flour.

Merlan whiting (*Merlangus merlangus*), a fish in the cod family named for its white, flaky flesh.

Messer knife.

Met mead.

Mettwurst raw pork sausage that is smoked or cured.

Metzger butcher.

Metzgerei butcher shop.

Miesmuscheln blue mussel (*Mytilus edulis*).

Milchladen dairy store.

Milchprodukte dairy produce.

Milchpulver powdered milk.

Milchschokolade milk chocolate.

Milchsuppe milk soup.

Mineralwasser mineral water, which usually is carbonated.

Minze mint.

Mischbrot brown bread.

mit Kohlensäure versetzt carbonated.

Mittagessen lunch.

Mohn poppy seed.

Molke whey.

Mungobohnen mung bean.

Muschel mussel.

Muschelfleisch scallop meat.

Muskatnuss nutmeg.

Muskelmagen gizzard.

Nachmittagstee afternoon tea.

Nachspeise dessert. Also *Nachtisch*.

Nachtisch dessert. Also *Nachspeise*.

naschen nibble.

Naturreis brown rice.

Nektarine nectarine.

Niere kidney.

Nudel noodle.

Nudelholz rolling pin.

Nuß nut.

Oblatan edible wafer papers used when baking holiday cookies.

Obst fruit. Also known as *Frucht*.

Ochsenschwanz oxtail.

Ofen geröstet oven-roasted.

ohne Knochen boned.

Ökoladen store with organic foods. Also called *Bioladen*.

Öl oil.

Olivenöl olive oil.

Orangenmarmelade orange marmalade.

Orangensaft orange juice.

Ostseehering Baltic herring (*Clupea harengus membras*), a variety of herring in the Baltic Sea somewhat smaller than the Atlantic herring (*Culpea harengus harengus*).

Paniermehl bread crumbs. Also known as *geriebene Semmel*.

paniert breaded.

Paprika bell pepper.

Paranuss Brazil nut.

Pastinake parsnip.

Perlzwiebeln pearl onion.

Petersilie parsley.

Petersilienwurzel parsley root.

Pfannkuchen pancake.

Pfeffer pepper.

Pfefferwurst spicy, all-beef sausage, served as a sliced cold cut.

Pfifferlingen chanterelle mushroom (*Cantharellus cibarius*).

Pfirsich peach.

Pflanzenfett vegetable fat (a solid).

Pflanzenöl vegetable oil.

Pflaume plum; prune.

Pflaumenmus plum jam.

Pils pilsner; light beer.

Pilz mushroom.

Pilzsauce mushroom sauce or gravy.

Piment allspice.

Pinienkernen pine nut.

Plätzchen cookie.

pochiert poached.

pochiertes Ei poached egg.

Portulak purslane.

Preiselbeere cranberry.

preiswert inexpensive.

Preskopf head cheese, usually made with aspic and lean pork or beef cheek meat. It looks more like a meat jelly than a cheese; served as a sliced cold cut. Also known as *souse* when pickled in vinegar.

Puderzucker powdered sugar.

Puter turkey.

Quappe burbot (*Lota lota*), a cod-like freshwater fish.

Quark fresh cheese that looks like a thick yogurt. It is used in desserts, especially cheesecake.

Quitte quince.

Rapsöl rapeseed oil or canola oil.

Räucherlachs smoked salmon.

Rechnung bill or check. Also called *Scheck*.

Regenbogenforelle rainbow trout (*Salmo gairdneri*).

Rehfleisch deer meat; venison.

Rehfleisch Braten venison roast.

reif ripe.

Reis rice.

Rentier reindeer (*Rangifer tarandus*).

Rentierfleisch reindeer meat.

Rettich radish.

Rhabarber rhubarb.

Rinderbrühe beef bouillon.

Rinderbrust beef brisket.

Rinderfilet beef tenderloin.

Rindfleisch beef.

Rindswürstchen small sausages that are slightly smoked and made with beef in Frankfurt. Also called *Frankfurter, Wiener, Würstchen, Halberstädter* in Thuringia, and *Schübling* in Swabia.

Ringlotten greengage (*Prunus domestica insititia*), a yellow-green fruit related to a plum.

Rippchen pork ribs, spareribs.

Rippe rib.

Roggen rye.

Roggenbrot rye bread.

Roggenmehl rye flour.

roh raw.

Rohrzucker unrefined cane sugar.

Rohschinken dry-cured ham, similar to prosciutto.

Römersalat romaine lettuce or cos lettuce; also called *Lattich*.

Rosenkohl Brussels sprouts.

Rosinen raisin.

Rosmarin rosemary.

rot red.

Rotbarsch ocean perch; red fish (*Sebastes marinus*).

rote Beete red beet.

rote Zwiebel red onion.

Rotkohl red cabbage.

Rotwein red wine.

Rotweinessig red wine vinegar.

Rotwild red deer.

Rübe beet; turnip.

Rübenzucker beet sugar.

Rühreier scrambled eggs.

russischer Stör Russian sturgeon (*Acipenser gueldenstaedtii*).

Sahne cream.

Saibling brook trout or arctic char (*Salvelinus fontinalis, Salvelinus alpinus*); also called *Bachsaibling*.

Salat lettuce; salad.

Salbei sage.

Salz salt.

Salzkartoffeln boiled potatoes.

Samen kernel or seed.

Sardellen anchovies.

Sardinen sardines.

Saubohne broad bean.

sauer sour; pickled. Another word for *sauer* is *gebeizt*.

Sauerampfer sorrel.

Sauerbraten marinated pot roast.

Sauerkraut fermented cabbage served as a sausage condiment or side dish.

Sauermilch curdled milk; sour milk.

Sauerrahm sour cream.

Sauerteigbrot sourdough bread.

Schaft shank.

Schalentiere shellfish.

Schalotte shallot.

Schankbier draft beer. Also called *Fassbier.*

scharf hot, spicy.

Schaumfestiger mousse.

Scheck the bill or check. Also called *Rechnung.*

Scheibe Brot slice of bread.

Schellfisch haddock (*Melanogrammus aeglefinus*).

Schinken ham.

Schinkenwurst ham sausage, served as a sliced cold cut.

Schlagsahne whipped cream; whipping cream.

Schmalz fat or lard.

Schmand thick cream similar to crème fraîche or extra-heavy whipping cream.

Schmerlen rockling (*Enchelyopus cimbrius*), a fish in the cod family.

Schmorbraten pot roast.

Schnaps clear, colorless spirits, liquor.

Schnecke snail.

Schneehuhn rock or mountain ptarmigan (*Lagopus muta*), a game bird in the grouse family.

Schnellimbiss stand-up food stall.

schnitt cut; slice.

Schnittlauch chives.

Schnitzel a meat cutlet, typically veal, coated with bread crumbs and fried.

Schokolade chocolate.

Schübling small sausages that are slightly smoked in Swabia. Also called *Frankfurter, Wiener,* and *Würstchen, Halberstädter* in Thuringia, and *Rindswürstchen* when made with beef in Frankfurt.

Schürze apron.

Schüssel bowl; saucer.

Schwarten peelings; rinds.

Schwarzbier dark beer.

schwarzer Goldbrasse black sea bream (*Spondyliosoma cantharus*).

schwarzer Himbeere black raspberry.

schwarzer Johannisbeere black currant.

schwarzer Kaffee black coffee.

schwarzer Pfeffer black pepper.

schwarzer Walnuss black walnut.

Schwarzwurzel black salsify (*Scorzonera hispanica*), a long, thin root vegetable with black skin and white flesh.

Schwein pig.

Schweinefleisch pork.

Schweinshaxe grilled pork hock.

Schweizer Käse Swiss cheese.

Schwertfisch swordfish.

Seeigel sea urchin (*Echinus esculentus*).

Seelachs saithe or coalfish (*Pollachius virens*), a member of the cod family.

Seetang kelp; seaweed.

Seeteufel anglerfish; monkfish (*Lophius piscatorius*).

Seezunge sole (*Solea vulgaris*), a flatfish.

Sekt sparkling wine.

Sellerie celery, celery root, or celeriac.

Selleriesamen celery seed.

Semmel roll.

Semmelbrösel bread crumbs.

Senf mustard.

Serviette napkin.

Sesamöl sesame oil.

Sesamsamen sesame seed.

Sodawasser soda water.

Sojabohnen soybean.

Solberfleisch boiled pickled beef.

Sonnenblumenkerne sunflower seed.

Sonnenblumenöl sunflower oil.

Soße gravy, sauce, or salad dressing.

Souse pickled head cheese. See *Preskopf.*

Spanferkel suckling pig.

Spargel asparagus.

Spätzle handmade noodles or dumplings.

Spätzle Hobel a planing device for scraping dough into boiling water to make the tiny noodles or dumplings called *Spätzle.*

Speck bacon.
Speisekarte menu.
Speiseöl cooking oil.
Spiegelei fried egg.
Spinat spinach.
Spirituosen spirits.
Spitzenkoch executive chef.
Stachelbeere gooseberry.
Stachelbeermarmelade gooseberry jam.
Steckrübe rutabaga or swede (*Brassica naps var. napobrassica*).
Steinbutt turbot (*Psetta maxima*).
Steinpilz porcini mushroom (*Boletus edulis*).
Sternanis star anise (*Illicium verum*).
stilles Wasser still water (not carbonated).
Stint smelt fish.
Stör sturgeon (*Acipenser stellatus*).
Streitkolben mace.
Suppe des Tages soup of the day.
Suppenlöffel soup spoon.
süß sweet.
süßer Wein sweet wine; dessert wine.
süßes Brötchen sweet bun.
Süßigkeiten candy; sweets.
Süßkartoffel sweet potato.
Süßspeisen desserts or sweet dishes.
Süßwasser Brassen freshwater bream (*Abramis ballerus*).
Süßwasserfische freshwater fish.
Süßwasserkrebse freshwater crayfish; also called *Flusskrebs* or *Languste*.

Tafelapfel eating apple.
Tafelwein table wine (but lower quality).
Tasse cup.
Teewurst a mildly sour, minced pork-beef sausage that is smoked, fermented, and air-dried.
Teig pastry; dough.
Teller plate.
Thunfisch tuna.

131

Thymian thyme.
Tiefseegarnelen deep-water prawns; northern shrimp (*Pandalus borealis*).
Tintenfisch squid; cuttlefish (*Sepiola atlantica*).
Tisch table.
Tischdecke tablecloth.
Topinambur Jerusalem artichoke.
traditionelles Essen traditional food.
Traube grape.
Trinken drink.
Trinkgeld tip; gratuity.
Trinkgeld inklusive tipping included.
Trinkwasser drinking water.
trocken dry.

unentgeltlich unappetizing.
ungezuckert unsweetened.
unreif unripe.
Untersetzer table mat, coaster.
Untertasse saucer.

Vanilleschote vanilla pod; vanilla bean.
Vegetarier vegetarian (noun).
vegetarisch vegetarian (adjective).
verdünnen dilute.
verglast glazed.
Vollkornbrot whole-wheat bread.
Vollmilch whole milk.
Vorspeise appetizer; starter.

Wacholderbeere juniper berry.
Wachs Bohne wax bean.
Wachtel quail.
Walderdbeere wild strawberry.
Walnuss walnut.
Walnussöl walnut oil.

Wasser water.

Wassermelone watermelon.

Wegerich plantain.

weich gekochtes Ei soft-boiled egg.

Wein wine.

Weinbrand brandy.

Weinkarte wine list.

Weinstein cream of tartar.

weiß white.

Weißbrot white bread.

weiße Goldbrasse white sea bream.

weiße Kopfkohl white head cabbage (*Brassica oleracea var. alba*).

weiße Schokolade white chocolate.

weiße Soße white sauce or gravy.

weiße Walnuss butternut or white walnut (*Juglans cinerea*).

weiße Zwiebel white onion.

weißen Bohne white bean; navy bean.

weißer Pfeffer white pepper.

weißer Spargel white asparagus.

Weißwein white wine.

Weißwurst mildly seasoned, white, veal-pork sausage, served hot and with sweet mustard for breakfast. A Munich specialty.

Weizen wheat.

Weizenbock ale made with mainly wheat malt.

Weizenbrot wheat bread.

Weizenkeim wheat germ.

Weizenmehl wheat flour.

Wels catfish.

Wiener small sausages that are slightly smoked. They can be made with beef, pork or poultry. Also called *Frankfurter, Würstchen, Halberstädter* in Thuringia, *Schübling* in Swabia, and *Rindswürstchen* when made with beef in Frankfurt.

Wildbret game.

Wildkaninchen wild rabbit.

Wintergrün wintergreen.

Wirsing Savoy cabbage.

Wolfsbarsch sea bass (*Dicentrarchus labrax* or *Morone labrax*).

Wurst sausage.

Wurst aus Schweinefleisch pork sausage.

Würstchen small sausages that are slightly smoked. They can be made with beef, pork, or poultry. Also called *Frankfurter, Wiener, Halberstädter* in Thuringia, *Schübling* in Swabia, and *Rindswürstchen* when made with beef in Frankfurt.

Wurzelgemüse root vegetable.

Würzmittel seasonings.

Zander pike-perch (*Sander spp.*), a genus of fish in the perch family that resembles the unrelated pike.

Zichorienkaffee a hot beverage made with roasted chicory.

Ziege goat. Also known as *Geiß*.

Ziegenmilch goat milk.

Zimt cinnamon.

Zitrone lemon.

Zitronenschale lemon zest.

Zuchtfisch farmed fish.

Zucker sugar.

Zucker Snap Erbse sugar snap pea.

Zuckerguss icing; frosting.

Zuckerrüben sugar beet.

Zunge tongue.

Zwetsche plum. Also spelled *Zwetschge*.

Zwiebel onion.

Zwiebelkuchen a bacon–onion tart, popular in autumn.

Zwiebelpulver onion powder.

Food Establishments

A Quick Reference Guide to Restaurants Visited

Research for this book involved many food establishments in Germany. Chefs are listed in *Acknowledgements*, and some of their recipes appear in *Tastes of Germany*. The telephone country code for Germany is 49. (You must first dial 011 from the U.S. for international calls.) Unlike a standard seven-digit U.S. phone number, German phone numbers may have up to ten digits; this includes up to five digits for a city's phone code, which follows the country code. Although individual listings traditionally appear in pairs (example: 22 34 78 76), other configurations have been used in more recent years.

Restaurants

Apfelwein Dax Willemerstraße 11, 60594 Frankfurt am Main
Tel (49) 69 61 64 37   www.apfelwein-dax.de
info@apfelwein-dax.de

Auerbachs Keller Grimmaische Strasse 2–4, 04109 Leipzigj
Tel (49) 341 21 61 00   www.auerbachs-keller-leipzig.de
info@auerbachs-keller-leipzig.de

Backerei und Café Gundel Hauptstraße 212, 69117 Heidelberg
Tel (49) 62 21 20 66 1   www.gundel-heidelberg.de
geschmack@gundel-heidelberg.de

Bautzener Senfrestaurant Schloßstraße 3, 02625 Bautzen
Tel (49) 35 91 59 80 15   www.senf-stube.de
info@senf-stube.de

Brauhaus Johannes Albrecht Adolphsbrücke 7, 20457 Hamburg
Tel (49) 40 36 77 40   www.brauhaus-joh-albrecht.de
hamburg@brauhaus-joh-albrecht.de

Breuer's Rüdesheimer Schloss Drosselgasse, D-65385 Rüdesheim am Rhein, Rheingau Tel (49) 67 22 90 50 0 www.ruedesheimer-schloss.com info@ruedesheimer-schloss.com

Bülow Palais & Residenz, Caroussel Restaurant Königstraße 14, 01097 Dresden Tel (49) 351 80 03 0 www.buelow-hotels.de info.palais@buelow-hotels.de

Café Elbterrassen Övelgönne 1, 22605 Hamburg Tel (49) 40 39 03 44 3 www.cafe-elbterrassen.de info@cafe-elbterrassen.de

Café Maldaner Marktstraße 34, 65183 Wiesbaden Tel (49) 611 30 52 14 www.cafe-maldaner.de cafemaldaner@t-online.de

The Cooking Ape Walther-von-Cronberg-Platz 2–4, 60594 Frankfurt Tel (49) 69 26 95 28 40 www.the-cooking-ape.com info@the-cooking-ape.com

Deidesheimer Hof am Marktplatz 67146 Deidesheim Tel (49) 6326 96 87 0 www.deidesheimerhof.de info@deidesheimerhof.de

Doctor Weinstuben Hebegasse 5, 54470 Bernkastel-Kues / Mosel Tel (49) 6531 96 65 0 www.doctor-weinstuben.de info@doctor-weinstuben.de

Fassbender and Rausch Chocolates Schokoladencafé am Gendarmenmarkt Charlottenstraße 60, 10117 Berlin Tel (49) 30 20 45 84 43 www.fassbender-rausch.com

Fischküche Laboe Inh. Harald Bruhn Hafenplatz, 24235 Laboe Tel (49) 4343 42 97 99 www.fischkueche-laboe.de fischkueche-laboe@t-online.de

Gugelhof Kollwitzplatz/Ecke Knaackstraße 37, 10435 Berlin Tel (49) 30 44 29 22 9 www.gugelhof.de gugelhof@t-online.de

Habel Weinkultur am Reichstag Luisenstraße 19, 10117 Berlin Tel (49) 30 28 09 84 84 www.wein-habel.de

Historische Wurstküchl Thundorferstraße 3, 93047 Regensburg Tel (49) 941 46 62 10 www.wurstkuchl.de info@wurstkuchl.de

Hofbräuhaus München Platzl 9, 80331 München Tel (49) 89 29 01 36 10 www.hofbraeuhaus.de hbteam@hofbraeuhaus.de

Hotel Bareiss Gärtenbühlweg 14, 72270 Baiersbronn-Mitteltal Tel (49) 7442 47 0 www.bareiss.com info@bareiss.com

Hotel Michaelis Paul-Gruner-Straße 44, 04107 Leipzig
Tel (49) 341 26 78 0 www.michaelis-leipzig.de
info@michaelis-leipzig.de

Hotel Sackmann 72270 Baiersbronn-Schwarzenberg
Tel (49) 7447 28 90 www.hotel-sackmann.de
info@hotel-sackmann.de

Hotel Traube Tonbach Tonbachstraße 237, 72270 Baiersbronn
Tel (49) 7442 49 20 www.traube-tonbach.de
info@traube-tonbach.de

Hotel zum Ritter St. Georg Hauptstraße 178, 69117 Heidelberg
Tel (49) 6221 13 50 www.ritter-heidelberg.de
info@ritter-heidelberg.de

Linslerhof Linslerhof 1, 66802 Überherrn
Tel (49) 6836 80 70 www.linslerhof.de
info@linslerhof.de

Louf Reventlouallee 2, 24105 Kiel
Tel (49) 431 55 11 78 www.louf.de/index.html

Radeberger Spezialausschank Terrassenufer 1, 01067 Dresden (Altstadt)
Tel (49) 351 48 48 66 0 www.radeberger-spezialausschank.de
info@radeberger-spezialausschank.de

Radisson Blu Schwarzer Bock Hotel Kranzplatz 12, 65183 Wiesbaden
Tel (49) 611 15 50 www.radissonblu.com
reservations.wiesbaden@radissonblu.com/hotel-wiesbaden

Ratskeller Kiel Fleethörn 9-11, 24103 Kiel
Tel (49) 431 97 10 00 5 www.ratskeller-kiel.de

Ratskeller München Marienplatz 8, 80331 München
Tel (49) 89 21 99 89 0 www.ratskeller.com
info@ratskeller.com

Restaurant Gargantua Park Gallery, An der Welle 3, 60322 Frankfurt am Main Tel. (49) 69 72 07 18 www.gargantua.de
info@gargantua.de

Restaurant Kastell at Hotel Burg Wernberg Schlossberg 10, 92533 Wernberg Tel (49) 9604 93 90 www.burg-wernberg.de
hotel@burg-wernberg.de

Schanzenstern Bartelsstraße 12, 20357 Hamburg
Tel (49) 40 43 29 04 09 www.schanzenstern.de
gasthaus@schanzenstern.de

Schiffercafé Kiel-Holtenau Alexander Stieler, Tiessenkai 9, 24159 Kiel
Tel (49) 431 90 89 67 6 www.schiffcafe-kiel.de
schiffercafe.kiel@yahoo.de

Schiffergesellschaft Breite Straße 2, 23552 Lübeck
Tel (49) 451 76 77 0 www.schiffergesellschaft.com

Schnookeloch Hotel and Restaurant Haspelgasse 8, 69117 Heidelberg
Tel (49) 6221 13 80 80   www.schnookeloch.de
kontakt@schnookeloch.de/restaurant.html
Sorbisches Restaurant Wjelbik Kornstraße 7, 02625 Bautzen
Tel (49) 3591 42 06 0   www.wjelbik.de
Zum Roten Ochsen Hauptstraße 217 am Karlsplatz, 69117 Heidelberg
Tel (49) 6221 20 97 7   www.roterochsen.de
info@roterochsen.de

Other Businesses

Alois Dallmayr Dienerstraße 14–15, 80331 München
Tel (49) 89 21 35 13 0   www.dallmayr.com
info@dallmayr.de
Deutsches Currywurst Museum Schützenstraße 70, 10117 Berlin
Tel (49) 30 88 71 86 47   www.currywurstmuseum.com
info@currywurstmuseum.com
KaDeWe Berlin Kaufhaus des Westens, Tauentzienstraße 21–24, 10789
Berlin   Tel (49) 30 21 21 20 55   www.kadewe.de
info@kadewe.de
Kleinmarkthalle Hasengasse 5–7, 60311 Frankfurt
Tel (49) 69 21 23 36 96   www.kleinmarkthalle.de
Niederegger Breite Straße 89, 23552 Lübeck
Tel (49) 451 53 01 12 6   www.niederegger.de
info@niederegger.de

Bibliography

Adam, Hans Karl. *The International Wine and Food Society's Guide to German Cookery.* London: International Wine and Food Society Publishing Co., 1971.

Anderson, Jean and Hedy Würz. *The New German Cookbook: More than 230 Contemporary and Traditional Recipes.* New York: HarperCollins, 1993.

Biró, Marcel and Shannon Kring Biró. *Biró: European-Inspired Cuisine.* Layton, UT: Gibbs Smith, 2005.

Bock, Hieronymus. *Kräuterbuch.* Germany: Gedruckt zü Strassburg, 1577.

Bonne, Josephine. *The Continental Cook Book: One Thousand and One Recipes of European Tradition.* New York: Minton, Blach and Co., 1928.

Davidis, Henriette. *Pickled Herring and Pumpkin Pie: A Nineteenth Century Cookbook for German Immigrants to America.* Madison, WI: Max Kade Institute for German American Studies, 2003.

Einhorn, Barbara. *West German Food and Drink.* New York: Bookwright Press, 1989.

Endress, Angela Francisca and Barbara Nickerson. *Original Hessich: The Best of Hessian Food.* Stuttgart, Germany: Walter Hädecke Verlag, 2010.

Goldstein, Darra and Kathrin Merkle, editors. *Culinary Cultures of Europe: Identity, Diversity and Dialogue.* Council of Europe Publishing, 2005.

Grimm, Jacob and Wilhelm Grimm. *The Complete Grimm's Fairy Tales.* New York: Pantheon Books, 1976.

Hassani, Nadia. *Spoonfuls of Germany: Culinary Delights of the German Regions in 170 Recipes.* New York: Hippocrene Books, 2007.

Hazelton, Nike Standen. *The Cooking of Germany.* New York: Time-Life Books, 1969.

Heinzelmann, Ursula. *Food Culture in Germany.* Westport, CT: Greenwood Press, 2008.

Hirst, Mike. *Germany.* Austin, TX: Raintree Steck-Vaughn, 2000.

Howe, Robin. *German Cooking.* Worcester, England: Ebenezer Baylis and Son Ltd., 1953.

Jacob, H. E. *Six Thousand Years of Bread: Its Holy and Unholy History.* New York: Skyhorse Publishing, 2007.

Kruger, Arne. *German Cooking: Savory German Dishes Prepared in the Traditional Way*. New York: Round the World Books Inc., 1976.

Loewen, Nancy. *Food In Germany*. Vero Beach, FL: Rourke Publications, 1991.

Marchello, Martin and Julie Garden-Robinson. *The Art and Process of Sausage Making*. Fargo, ND: North Dakota State University Extension Service, 2012.

Meier, Mrs. Lina. *The Art of German Cooking and Baking*. Milwaukee: Wetzel Brothers Printing Co., 1937.

Northcott, Kenneth. *A Literary History of Germany*. London: Bow Historical Books, 1975.

Oetker, August. *German Cooking Today: The Original*. Bielefeld, Germany: Dr. Oetker Verlag, 2006.

Ostmann, Barbara Gibbs. *The Recipe Writer's Handbook*. Hoboken, NJ: John Wiley & Sons, 2011.

Parnell, Helga. *Cooking the German Way*. Minneapolis: Lerner Publications Company, 1988.

Passant, E. J. *A Short History of Germany: 1815–1945*. Cambridge, England: Cambridge University Press, 1959.

Pool, Jim. *Rations of the German Wehrmacht in World War II*. Atglen, PA: Schiffer Publishing Ltd, 2007; *Volume 2*, 2012.

Reagin, Nancy R. *Sweeping the German Nation: Domesticity and National Identity in Germany, 1870–1945*. Cambridge, England: Cambridge University Press, 2007.

Ruhlman, Michael. *Ratio: The Simple Codes Behind the Craft of Everyday Cooking*. New York: Scribner, 2010.

Scharfenberg, Horst. *The Cuisines of Germany: Regional Specialties and Traditional Home Cooking*. New York: Poseidon Press, 1989.

Wason, Betty. *The Art of German Cooking*. New York: Doubleday, 1967.

Weiss, Hans U. Gastronomia: Eine Bibliographie der Deutschsprachigen Gastronomie 1485–1914. Zurich, Switzerland: Bibliotheca Gastronomia, 1996.

Wheaton, Barbara Ketcham. *Savoring the Past: The French Kitchen and Table from 1300 to 1789*. Philadelphia: The University of Pennsylvania Press, 1983.

Online sources

GermanBeerInstitute.com

GermanFoodGuide.com

Germany.travel

KitchenProject.com

KitchenDaily.com

WorldAtlas.com

Index

allspice *Piment* 33, 40, 104, 126
almond *Mandel* 6, 33, 36, 41, 90, 92,
    96, 100, 103, 106, 111–112,
    124
anchovies *Sardellen* 18, 96, 100, 107,
    128
apple *Apfel* 2, 11, 18, 20–21, 23,
    28–30, 32, 34, 38, 75, 90–92,
    94, 96, 98–100, 105–106, 108,
    110, 113–114, 116, 122, 131
apricot *Aprikose* 107, 114
artichoke *Artischocken* 114, 132
asparagus *Spargel* 18, 25, 35, 38, 40,
    75, 80, 92, 99, 109, 130, 133

bacon *Speck* 12, 20–21, 25, 37, 39–40,
    91–98, 100–102, 104–107,
    110–111, 118, 131, 134
barley *Gerste* 2, 3, 111, 119
basil *Basilikum* 114
bay leaf *Lorbeerblatt* 124
bean *Bohne* 92, 98, 111, 115,
    117–119, 122, 124–125, 128,
    130, 132–133
    sprouts *Bohnensprossen* 115
beef *Rindfleisch* 18, 21, 24–26, 32–37, 91,
    93, 95–97, 100, 103–107, 109–111,
    114, 117, 120, 122–123, 126–127,
    129–131, 133–134
beer *Bier* 3–4, 8, 15, 18, 23, 26, 29, 32,
    34–35, 37, 39, 41, 75, 78, 88–89,
    92–93, 100, 105, 109, 111, 113–
    115, 117, 120, 124, 126, 129, 133

beet *Rübe* 18, 22, 33–34, 38, 87, 90,
    99, 102, 106, 109, 128, 134
berry *Beere* 92, 106, 114, 132
blackberry *Brombeere* 115
blueberry *Blaubeere* 92, 99, 115, 120
borage *Borretsch* 115
brandy *Schnapps* 27, 108, 118, 122, 133
brain *Gehirn* 99, 118
bread *Brot* 3, 7, 11–12, 14, 18–20, 29,
    32–33, 36–38, 87–94, 96–112,
    115, 117, 119, 122–123,
    125–126, 128–130, 132–133
broccoli *Brokkoli* 115
Brussels sprouts *Rosenkohl* 128
buckwheat *Buchweizen* 38, 93, 104, 115

cabbage *Kohl* 6, 18, 22, 29–31, 35,
    90–91, 97, 100–102, 106–107,
    110–111, 122, 128–129, 133
cake *Kuchen* 10, 17–18, 27, 29, 34,
    41–42, 76, 88, 90–94, 96,
    98, 101, 104–109, 112–113,
    122–123
candy *Süßigkeiten* 29, 31, 41, 103, 131
caraway *Kümmel* 25, 34, 98, 102–103, 123
carrot *Karotte* 21, 28, 30, 36, 38, 105,
    110, 121
cauliflower *Blumenkohl* 36, 115
celery; celeriac *Sellerie* 29, 92, 130
cheese *Käse* 2, 5–6, 14, 18–19, 25, 29–
    30, 34, 87–88, 90, 92–93, 95–98,
    101–105, 110–111, 115–116,
    118, 121–122, 124, 127, 130

cherry *Kirsche* 18, 27–28, 90–91,
100–101, 108, 111, 122
chervil *Kerbel* 101, 122
chicken *Hähnchen* 5–6, 88, 91–93,
96–97, 99, 102, 120–121
chickpea *Kichererbse* 122
chives *Schnittlauch* 23, 38, 129
chocolate *Schokolade* 14, 18, 25,
27–29, 31, 33, 35, 37, 41–42,
76, 96, 105, 107–108, 120,
125, 129, 133
cinnamon *Zimt* 6, 24, 29, 33, 39, 43,
90–92, 96, 100–103, 108, 111,
134
clam *Ensis* 117
clove *Gewürznelken* 24, 33, 39, 102,
104, 119
coconut *Kokosnuss* 101, 122
coffee *Kaffee* 14, 42, 87–88, 91, 93,
105, 107, 121, 130
cold cut *Aufschnitt* 87–88, 114–115,
118–119, 124, 126–127, 129
coleslaw *Krautsalat* 123
cookies *Plätzchen* 24, 87, 90, 92–93,
99, 101, 104, 106, 109, 111,
126
corn *Mais* 15, 113, 124
cornmeal *Maismehl* 124
cottage cheese *Hüttenkäse* 18, 103,
121
crab *Krabbe* 38, 98, 123
cranberry *Preiselbeere* 35, 93, 127
crawfish; crayfish *Flusskrebs* 103, 117,
123, 131
cucumber *Gurke* 18, 31, 38, 45, 98,
108–109, 115, 119
cumin *Kreuzkümmel* 29, 123
currant *Johannisbeere* 23, 106, 114,
121, 130
cuttlefish *Tintenfisch* 132

dessert *Nachspeise* 10, 17, 36, 43, 88,
91, 104–105, 107–111, 125,
127, 131
duck *Ente* 30, 88, 95–96, 116

dumplings *Spätzle* 6, 9, 12, 18,
20–21, 29–30, 35, 88, 91–103,
106–107, 109–112, 122–130

eel *Aal* 6, 37, 39, 75, 90, 98, 113
egg *Ei* 8, 24, 26, 29, 36, 41, 76, 88,
90–105, 107–111, 116–117,
119–120, 127–128, 131, 133
white *Eiweiß* 116
yolk *Eigelb; Dotter* 116
eggplant *Aubergine* 90, 114
elderberry *Holunderbeere* 96, 120
elk *Elch* 116

fennel *Fenchel* 117
fenugreek *Bockshornklee* 115
fig *Feige* 6, 28, 117
fish *Fisch* 7–8, 14, 21–22, 25, 28,
31–32, 38–40, 75–76,
88–89, 95–101, 104, 108–111,
114–115, 117–120, 121–125,
127–131, 133–134
roe *Fischrogen* 117
frankfurter *Frankfurter* 19, 110
frog's legs *Froschschenkel* 118
fruit *Frucht; Obst* 3, 12, 14, 18, 21,
30, 34, 38–39, 41, 75, 85,
87–93–96, 98–110, 116,
118–119, 126–127

game *Wildbret* 28, 129, 133
garden cress *Kresse* 123
garlic *Knoblauch* 114, 122
ginger *Ingwer* 6, 28, 33, 71, 118, 121
gingerbread *Lebkuchen* 24, 33–34,
36, 90, 93, 95, 100, 102, 104,
111, 124
gizzard *Muskelmagen* 125
goose *Gans* 8, 20, 61, 88, 96, 118
gooseberry *Stachelbeere* 90, 98, 131
grape *Traube* 3, 132
grouse *Raufußhuhn* 114, 120, 129
gruel *Haferschleim* 3, 5, 98, 111, 120

ham *Schinken* 15, 19, 21–22, 27, 29, 31–32, 40, 88–89, 91–92, 96, 101–102, 109, 118–119, 128, 129
hare *Hase* 94–95, 120
hazelnut *Haselnuss* 24, 99, 120
head cheese *Preskopf* 110, 127, 130
heart *Herz* 13, 76, 110–111, 114, 120
herring *hering* 18, 37–39, 75, 89, 91, 93–94, 99, 102–103, 106–107, 109, 111, 116–117, 119, 124, 126
honey *Honig* 10, 14, 20, 33, 90–92, 99, 109, 121
hops *Hopfen* 26, 32, 121
horseradish *Kren* 20, 26, 34, 5–36, 95, 103, 106, 108, 110, 123–124

ice cream *Eis* 27, 106–107, 109, 116

jam *Konfitür* 91, 102, 104, 123, 126, 131
jelly *Gelee* 21, 28, 34, 118–119, 127
Jerusalem artichoke *Topinambur* 132
juice *Saft* 90–91, 95, 98, 106, 114, 118–119, 123, 126
juniper berry *Wacholderbeere* 32, 40, 132

kale *Grünkohl* 20, 39, 98, 105, 119
kidney *Niere* 13, 30, 107, 118, 125

lamb *Lamm* 5, 8, 35, 94, 98–99, 107, 116, 123
lard *Schmalz* 129
leek *Lauch* 95, 110–111, 123
lemon *Zitrone* 32, 36, 90–91, 94–95, 98, 102, 111, 118, 134
lentil *Linsen* 2, 12, 103, 110
lettuce *Salat* 31, 102, 115–116, 123, 128
lingonberry *Preiselbeere* 93
liqueur *Likör* 124
liquor *Alkohol* 89, 129, 133

liver *Leber* 19, 24, 29–30, 95–96, 100, 102–103, 107, 109, 115, 119, 121, 124
paté *Leberpastete* 102
lobster *Hummer* 37, 89, 96, 99, 121
lovage *Liebstöckel* 124

mace *Streitkolben* 39, 131
marjoram *Majoran* 24, 124
marmalade *Marmelade* 87, 123, 126
marzipan *Marzipan* 15, 17, 27–28, 33, 39, 41, 73, 92, 103, 124
meat *Fleisch* 4–5, 7–9, 13–15, 17, 19–23, 25–29, 30–32, 36, 38, 40, 79–80, 88, 90–91, 94–95, 97–98, 100–110, 115–121, 124–125, 127, 129
meatball *Frikadelle* 36, 39, 95, 99, 102, 115, 118
meringue *Baiser* 114
milk *Milch* 3, 6, 14, 18, 25–26, 29–30, 34, 38, 41, 90, 93, 95, 103, 106, 108, 117, 124–125, 129, 132, 134
millet *Hirse* 3, 120
mint *Minze* 118, 125
moose *Elch* 116
mousse *Schaumfestiger* 18, 91–92, 95, 111, 129
mulberry *Maulbeere* 124
mushroom *Pilz* 18, 38, 92–93, 100, 102–103, 105–106, 116, 126, 131
mussel *Muschel* 103–104, 125
mustard *Senf* 20, 22–23, 28, 33, 39, 92, 94, 109, 114, 130, 133
mutton *Hammelfleisch* 97, 120

nectarine *Nektarine* 125
nut *Nuß* 33, 95, 101, 116, 125–126, 130
nutmeg *Muskatnuss* 6, 24, 39, 97, 100–102, 118, 125–126

oats *Hafer* 3, 105, 117, 120
octopus *Krake* 123

offal *Innereien* 9, 19, 121
oil *Öl* 42, 116, 124, 126–127, 30–132
onion *Zwiebel* 18, 29, 32, 35, 38, 118,
    123, 126, 128, 133–134
orange *Orange* 24, 28, 36
oxtail *Ochsenschwanz* 126
oyster *Auster* 90, 97, 110, 114

pancake *Pfannkuchen* 7, 9, 23, 90,
    93–95, 100, 102, 104–106, 109,
    126
parsley *Petersilie* 95, 98, 100, 104,
    110, 118, 126
parsley root *Petersilienwurzel* 110, 126
parsnip *Pastinake* 126
pea *Erbse* 2, 12, 38, 93, 95, 116, 118,
    134
    sugar snap *Zucker Snap Erbse* 134
peach *Pfirsich* 126
peanut butter *Erdnussbutter* 116
pear *Birne* 17, 21, 34, 36, 39, 92–93,
    96, 98–99, 101, 114
pepper *Pfeffer* 28, 39–40, 95, 116,
    119, 126, 130, 133
    bell *Paprika* 99, 103, 107, 111, 126
pickle *Essiggurke* 18, 23, 34, 91, 95,
    99, 106–107, 117, 119
pineapple *Ananas* 113
plum *Pflaume* 23, 27, 96, 105, 112,
    118, 126–127, 134
pomegranate *Granatapfel* 119
poppy seed *Mohn* 17, 103, 125
pork *Schweinefleisch* 2, 5, 15, 18–21,
    24–25, 28–29, 33, 35–38, 40,
    79, 91, 93–101, 103–109, 111,
    114–115, 117, 120, 122–125,
    127–128, 130–131, 133–134
porridge *Haferbrei* 7, 120
potato *Erdapfel* 10, 13, 18, 20–21, 23,
    25, 28–30, 32, 34–36, 38–40,
    88, 91–102, 104–112, 116,
    119, 122, 128, 131
poultry *Geflügel* 88, 96, 117–118,
    120, 133–134

pretzel *Brezel* 20, 23, 33, 88, 92–93,
    102, 115, 123
prune *Pflaume* 20, 96, 98, 103, 112,
    126
pumpkin *Kürbis* 94, 102, 123
purslane *Portulak* 127

quail *Wachtel* 132
quince *Quitte* 127

rabbit *Kaninchen* 3, 8, 14, 99, 121, 133
radish *Rettich* 106, 127
raisin *Rosinen* 87, 90, 92, 96, 99–101,
    106, 110–111, 128
raspberry *Himbeere* 92, 120, 130
reindeer *Rentier* 127
rhubarb *Rhabarber* 90, 106, 127
rice *Reis* 88, 90, 97, 103, 106, 121,
    125, 127
roll *Semmel* 87–88, 93, 98, 108–109,
    115, 120, 123, 130
rosemary *Rosmarin* 128
rutabaga *Steckrübe* 13, 131
rye *Roggen* 5, 32, 36, 38, 91, 96,
    98–99, 101, 104, 106, 111,
    117, 119, 128

sage *Salbei* 107, 128
salad *Salat* 8, 18, 22–23, 28–30,
    38–39, 88, 92, 94, 96, 98–99,
    101–102, 104, 106, 109, 111,
    115, 122, 128, 130
salsify, black *Schwarzwurzel* 130
salt *Salz* 128
sardines *Sardinen* 128
sauce *Soße* 12, 17, 20–22, 27, 32,
    35–36, 38–39, 87, 90–100,
    102–111, 113, 115–116, 119,
    126, 130, 133
sauerkraut *Kraut; Sauerkraut* 6, 12,
    18, 20–21, 23, 29–30, 32, 39,
    50–51, 91, 97, 105, 107–108,
    110–111
sausage *Wurst* 5, 7, 9, 15, 18–21,
    23–26, 32–33, 36–37, 39,

75–77, 79, 87–89, 91, 93–94,
98–101, 105, 108–111, 113–120,
122–127, 129, 131, 133–134
scallion *Frühlingszwiebel* 118, 123
scallop *Jakobsmuschel* 106, 119, 121,
123–125
seasonings *Würzmittel* 90, 97,
103–104, 106–108, 134
sea urchin *Seeigel* 130
sesame seed *Sesamsamen* 130
shallot *Schalotte* 9, 129
shrimp *Tiefseegarnelen* 40, 93, 96,
102–103, 107, 132
smelt *Stint* 131
snail *Schnecke* 129
sorrel *Sauerampfer* 96, 129
soufflé *Auflauf* 90, 104, 114
soup *Suppe* 12, 18, 21–22, 28–29,
36, 38, 88–93, 95–102, 104,
106–111, 115–116, 121,
124–125, 131
sour cream *Sauerrahm* 40, 89, 91–92,
94, 98–99, 101, 105–106, 129
spearmint *Grüneminze* 119
spices *Gewürze* 6–7, 10, 12, 19, 24,
26, 33, 35–36, 39–41, 88–90,
94, 99, 104, 106–107, 110,
113, 119
spinach *Spinat* 100, 103, 109, 131
sprat *Sprotte* 109, 117
squid *Tintenfisch* 132
star anise *Sternanis* 131
stew *Eintopf* 6–8, 13, 18–19, 21–22,
38, 88, 90, 92, 95–96, 98–100,
105, 107–108, 111, 116
strawberry *Erdbeere* 95, 116, 132
stuffing *Füllung* 95, 97, 100, 108, 111,
118
sugar *Zucker* 6, 12–14, 27, 32–34, 36,
38, 40, 134
maple *Ahornzucker* 113
sugar beet *Zuckerrüben* 13, 33, 38, 87,
90, 134
sweetbreads *Kalbsbries* 121
sweet potato *Süßkartoffel* 131

Swiss chard *Mangold* 124
syrup *Sirup* 33–34, 87, 90, 92, 104, 113

tarragon *Estragon* 117
tea *Tee* 88, 116, 121, 123, 125
thyme *Thymian* 132
tomato *Tomate* 21, 35, 38–39,
92, 97–98, 100, 103, 106,
110–111, 116
tongue *Zunge* 102, 104, 110, 134
tumeric *Kurkuma* 123
turkey *Puter* 127
turnip *Rübe* 107, 109–111, 128

veal *Kalbfleisch* 18, 21, 23–24, 26, 36,
88, 95, 97, 100, 108, 110–111,
115, 118, 121, 129, 133
vegetable *Gemüse* 4–8, 10, 12, 21–22,
27, 30–31, 34–36, 38–39, 75,
85, 87–88, 91, 94, 97–99, 103,
105, 107–111, 116, 119, 126,
130, 134
venison *Rehfleisch* 5, 21, 27–28, 35,
105–107, 120, 127

watercress *Brunnenkresse* 115
watermelon *Wassermelone* 133
wheat *Weizen* 2, 23, 26, 88, 91–92,
106, 111, 117, 119–120,
132–133
whipped cream *Schlagsahne* 91, 95,
105–108, 111, 129
wine *Wein* 3–4, 6, 8, 15, 18, 28–30,
35, 43, 76, 81, 87–90, 92–100,
103, 106–112, 114, 120, 128,
130–133
wintergreen *Wintergrün* 133

yogurt *Joghurt* 94, 101, 116, 121, 127

H. 5/13

design   Ekeby
cover design   Susan P. Chwae
color printing   Traver Graphics, Inc.
book production   Sheridan Books, Inc.

typefaces   Garamond Simoncini and Helvetica Black
paper   60# House White